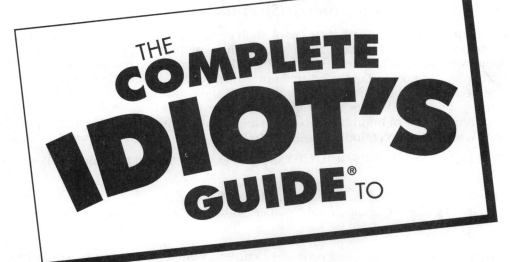

THE COMPLETE IDIOT'S GUIDE® TO

Tae Kwon Do

by Karen Eden and Keith Yates

alpha books

International Standard Book Number: 0-02862389-4
Library of Congress Catalog Card Number: 98-85971

05   04   03   8   7   6

Interpretation of the printing code: the rightmost number of the first series of numbers is the year of the book's printing; the rightmost number of the second series of numbers is the number of the book's printing. For example, a printing code of 98-1 shows that the first printing occurred in 1998.

Printed in the United States of America

Alpha Development Team

Publisher
Kathy Nebenhaus

Editorial Director
Gary M. Krebs

Managing Editor
Bob Shuman

Marketing Brand Manager
Felice Primeau

Senior Editor
Nancy Mikhail

Development Editors
Phil Kitchel
Jennifer Perillo
Amy Zavatto

Editorial Assistant
Maureen Horn

Production Team

Development Editor
Nancy Warner

Production Editor
Christy Wagner

Copy Editor
Martha Thieme

Technical Editor
Keith D. Yates

Cover Designer
Mike Freeland

Photo Editor
Richard H. Fox

Illustrators
Jody P. Schaeffer
Keith D. Yates

Designer
Glenn Larsen

Indexer
Tim Wright

Layout/Proofreading
Angela Calvert
Kim Cofer

Contents at a Glance

Contents

Foreword

When I first started teaching Tae Kwon Do in the United States in 1956, even I never dreamed the worldwide impact this unique martial art would have. I have seen countless lives—from inner-city youths to congressmen—literally changed through their training. Today Tae Kwon Do is a way of life for millions of people from Milwaukee to Moscow.

There are three kinds of people in the world. Those who make things happen, those who watch things happen, and those who don't even know what is happening. To make things happen, we must know how. Education is the key to making things happen and becoming a winner in life. Many people do not know about the benefits of the martial arts. That's why I am glad that experienced teachers like Ms. Eden and Master Yates have put together this book so students and prospective students can give themselves an education in this fascinating art of Tae Kwon Do.

I truly believe that the discipline and respect the martial arts teach can transform our society. Having proper goals and the discipline to accomplish them is an outgrowth of Tae Kwon Do studies. Having respect for yourself and others leads to an improved sense of self-confidence. In fact, my students' creed is "confidence through knowledge in the mind, honesty in the heart, and strength in the body."

During my 50-year search for truth through Tae Kwon Do practice, I have come to the conclusion that the human society will not improve unless parents and teachers practice a Lead by Example Action Philosophy—that is, teach children to achieve a human perfection by not making mistakes knowingly.

May God bless you in your training, and may you strive to become a living example to others. Together we can create a healthier and happier life for everyone.

—Grandmaster Jhoon Rhee

The "Father of Tae Kwon Do" in America (and the former Soviet Union)

Jhoon Rhee is perhaps the best known Tae Kwon Do practitioner in the United States. He introduced America to the Korean martial arts in 1956 and is recognized as the "Father of Tae Kwon Do" not only in the United States but also in the former Soviet Union. He changed the face of competition in this country with his introduction of padded sparring gear and with the invention of musical forms. He has appeared on the cover of *Parade* magazine and in every major martial arts publication. Grandmaster Rhee has taught in the Washington, D.C. area for many years, instructing many national champions and well as political leaders.

Introduction

Tae Kwon Do is said to be the most-practiced martial art in the Western world. It's definitely one of the *harder styles* of martial arts. That doesn't mean it's hard to learn, but that we do hard punches and kicks, as opposed to "soft" styles, like Tai Chi or Aikido.

In fact, kicking is what makes Tae Kwon Do unique among the many styles of martial arts. We like kicks. They're effective and fun to do. You don't have to be great at kicking to be an effective and successful Tae Kwon Doist, but you are going to learn to use your legs in a way that most people could never dream of. Don't worry. It's really not that difficult. All it takes is patience and a little self-discipline, two of the many things you'll be learning in your Tae Kwon Do training. But until then, let's not wait any longer!

What You'll Find in This Book

Part 1, "Your Intro to the Do," offers a great introduction to the martial arts in general and to Tae Kwon Do in particular. We'll list many of the obvious benefits and many of the not so obvious reasons you'd want to take up training.

We want you to know the mental as well as the physical aspects of the arts. That includes many intangible benefits that we'll spell out for you. We'll also tell you where Tae Kwon Do came from (the past) and where it's going (the future).

Once you've got a basic grasp of the martial arts its time to "Kick-Start Your Training," in Part 2. Here you'll find out how to find the best school and teacher for you or for your kids. You'll learn about what to expect on your first night. We'll fill you in on what to do, and perhaps more importantly, what *not* to do in a Tae Kwon Do class. We'll even tell you how to buy one of those cool martial arts outfits and how to put it on so you'll look the part right off.

Get ready to work in Part 3, "Making the Moves." Here's where the real fun begins as you start to learn the balances, kicks, blocks, and hand strikes. We'll describe them all in detail so you can practice on your own at home. We've included photos and drawings to make things easy to follow. You should be aware of the safety precautions to take in your training, either in the school or at home, and we'll cover them here.

Part 4, "Putting It All Together," does just what the title implies. We'll begin to take the basic techniques that we covered in Part 3 and we'll combine them and enlarge on them to help you do a little sparring practice. Sparring is the foundation of the sport of Tae Kwon Do and it serves as some of the best training for self-defense. And speaking of self-defense, this is the reason most students take up the martial arts. We'll look at the principles of defending yourself and your loved ones from unwanted aggressors.

Part 5, "Climbing the Ladder: Testing for Promotions," takes you step by step through what for many is the most frightening part of Tae Kwon Do, testing for a new belt color in front of a panel of judges. But not to worry, after you read this section you'll be ready to pass with flying colors. We'll also take a look at the mysterious and coveted black belt rank.

The fun really begins in Part 6, "The Wide, Wide World of Competition." Here we'll cover the many different types of sport Tae Kwon Do and martial arts you can get involved in. We'll talk about the benefits and the dangers of the competitive world. We'll teach you the rules and regulations and even give you some tips to help you earn your first trophy or medal.

Just when you think you must know everything there is to know about Tae Kwon Do we'll give you a listing of other resources like magazines and suppliers of training aids. We'll even provide you with a glossary of the most commonly used terms in the art and sport.

When you finish this book you won't be an expert—only a few years in the training hall will do that—but we guarantee you will know more than any other student on the mat about the intricacies and inner workings of this fascinating martial art from the "Land of the Morning Calm," Korea.

Extras

Along the way you'll encounter bits of information that make the book not only more readable but more personal and relevant. We think you'll find these bits and pieces extremely interesting. Here's what to look for:

Wise Sa Bum Tells Us

These boxes offer you tips and advice as you perfect your skills.

Know the Do
These boxes will give you definitions of some of the Korean or Japanese terms you'll encounter in your training.

Watch Out, Grasshopper
These cautionary boxes contain information on how to avoid potential problems.

Martial Arts Minute
These boxes offer some interesting tidbits and insights into the world of martial arts.

Acknowledgments

My deepest appreciation to my book mentor and good friend John Corcoran, whom without, this book project would not be possible. Also, I couldn't have made it without my co-author Master Keith Yates who did a fantastic job in every aspect.

Special thanks to Master Robert Zang and Mr. Tim Curci and students of Young Brothers Tae Kwon Do. And to Mr. Zak Szabo and students of C.S Kim Karate in Pittsburgh. Also, special thanks to martial arts financial guru John Graden of the National Association of Professional Martial Artists.

Finally, I could never pass on what I have learned if it weren't for my own instructors Master C.S Kim and Master Joe Bruno. I am in deepest gratitude for all you have taught me. I got lucky.

Part 1
Your Intro to the Do

Do literally means the *way* or the *path*. *When you start your training in Tae Kwon Do (the way of kicking and punching), you are embarking on a path that will be unlike anything you have ever undertaken. Here is an introduction to this most unique martial art. Tae Kwon Do is an ancient art form to be sure, but it is also perhaps the most modern of the many Asian styles. It is taught in practically every city and town in America and has become almost as recognizable as the generic term Karate.*

Chapter 1

Why Would You Want to Do Tae Kwon Do?

In This Chapter

➤ Taking up the martial arts

➤ Training in Tae Kwon Do today

➤ Discovering the physical benefits of Tae Kwan Do

➤ Understanding the *mental* and even *spiritual* aspects

➤ Finding the best instructor for your needs

It's probably due to television, movies, and video games, but the words *martial arts* conjure up images of philosophy-spouting avengers who wipe out gangs of criminals with little more than their empty hands and bare feet. But in spite of how many times you've seen Steven Seagal, Jackie Chan, or Chuck Norris effortlessly dispatch the bad guys, I have news for you—that's 90 percent *make believe* aided by camera angles and talented stuntmen. A real fight is much more complicated. I've known those who have success-fully mastered street fights, but I also know some real martial artists who, for various reasons, have gotten beat up in street fights, too.

Now I am not saying that martial arts aren't good for self-defense—they're great—it's just that any amount of lessons, even enough lessons to make you a black belt, won't guarantee a victory in a real fight. There is no magic technique, no easy, secret move that will make you superman or superwoman.

Actually, martial arts are anything but easy. Learning Tae Kwon Do, Karate, Judo, Kung Fu, or any of the other arts is hard, sweaty work. Like most anything worthwhile, becoming really good at this is going to take time and patience. It's going to cost you more than just tuition. It will cost you the evenings you used to spend in front of the TV and out with friends. You'll be discouraged. You'll get tired, maybe even feel your training is monotonous at times.

So Why Would You Want to Do This?

Why even bother with Tae Kwon Do? Actually the benefits themselves would take a whole book. And if you asked a thousand martial artists why they took up the arts you would get a thousand different answers. The funny thing is, the reason most people sign up is usually not the reason they choose to continue with their training.

As an instructor, I've heard everything from "Johnny needs more discipline," to "I wanna learn how to kick some butt!" After a few weeks of training, though, most people get a whole new perspective on this martial arts stuff. They start to realize things like *discipline evolves from self-respect*. And *it's not about kicking some butt*, it's actually about learning how to control your emotions in the first place.

Many adult students are attracted to martial arts because they're intrigued by the *internal* aspects they've heard such studies can develop. Let's face it, it takes a certain mind-set to even consider such training. Many are too intimidated to even dare walk in the door of a Karate or Tae Kwon Do school. As you will discover in these pages it doesn't take a special person to start Tae Kwon Do, but it does take a special person to stick with it. The good news is, Tae Kwon Do training makes you a special person.

> **Martial Arts Minute**
> There are many different martial arts ranging from the slow and graceful to the violently demanding. Tae Kwon Do falls somewhere in the middle. Maybe that is the reason it is the most popular martial art in the Western world (and in the whole world if you don't count those millions of Chinese people doing their Chinese styles, like Tai Chi, on street corners).

So Who's Doing the Do?

Most people think that those who sign up for Tae Kwon Do or Karate lessons do so because they are the scrawny ones, like those in the back of the comic books, always getting sand kicked in their faces. These are the guys who have something to prove because they were always getting beat up at the bus stop as a kid. Truthfully, there are some students like that—and by the way, nobody picks on them anymore—but the majority of students do not fit that stereotype.

4

Anyone from any walk of life may be a student of martial arts. Male and female, young and old, all races, and from every economic and social background you could imagine. I remember standing in front of class one morning and I couldn't believe the array of students lined up before me. There in the second row was one of our local police officers, an orange belt who had signed up to help alleviate job stress. Right next to him was a suspect in a local criminal case, also an orange belt who had signed up to get better control of his life. And if that wasn't enough, in the front row was an older lady, a red belt, and a relative of a recent crime victim. None of them knew each other's personal lives. All they knew was that they were there to train together with mutual respect.

That's another beauty about Tae Kwon Do—it doesn't really matter who you are or why you're there. You could be a doctor or a ditch digger, a Catholic or a Protestant, a Cowboy's fan or a Redskin's fan, or even a cop or a criminal. It doesn't matter; you are all there to learn the same lessons about yourself and about life. Your status in life is left outside the door of the school.

In addition, Tae Kwon Do and other martial arts are ageless. You could be a 65-year-old woman who hasn't done a thing since 10th-grade gym class and still have hopes of achieving black belt someday. Naturally you won't be as fast, or able to kick as high as a 16-year-old, but how slow you go or high you kick will not be the deciding factor in your becoming a black belt. In Tae Kwon Do, you go at your own pace, and you can train until you just physically can't train anymore.

These Tae Kwon Do students are in their 70s and 80s.

The Kick Butt Factor

Sure, there are those who sign up for the self-defense aspect, especially women. As I've just told you, you won't become a superhero, but you will learn how to handle yourself in a sticky situation. This skill will, of course, come with practice, but interestingly, so will the realization that you'll probably never have to use those skills for the purpose of self-defense. Most people tend not to act like victims after martial arts training. Of course, it is nice to know that you could handle yourself if the need should arise—and it's this knowledge that makes you a little more confident in almost all situations, not just walking down dark alleys. You and I know you aren't really going to grab that obnoxious, teenage clerk at the pizza place and give him a swift, turning back kick, but just the knowledge that you could gives you the patience to put up with him.

Author Karen Eden showing the self-defense aspects of Tae Kwon Do.

Wise Sa Bum Tells Us

According to police statistics, it's a fact that just being confident and walking more confident can actually make you less of a target for potential assault. It seems the average mugger or pickpocket always looks for the easiest and most vulnerable victims.

Being able to handle yourself in a less-than-desirable situation is something you just can't put a price on. You won't always have access to a weapon like a gun or mace, but your hands and feet will always be available. Being able to react automatically and instantaneously when threatened is the very reason the ancient monks first conceived of the idea of martial arts training to begin with.

Like it or not, in our society men are often seen as the "protectors" of their families. As a trained martial artist, you'll feel up to the task.

As a woman, there's not a greater feeling in the world than walking down the street and knowing that you can handle yourself should you become accosted. As a parent, there is tremendous peace of mind in knowing your children have been taught how to react should a stranger ever try to approach them.

The Kiddos

The majority of students in Tae Kwon Do schools these days are children under the age of 18. Some of these youngsters have wanted to train since they saw the *Power Rangers* or *Ninja Turtles*. But truth be told, a good majority of children are there because Mom and Dad are making them go—or possibly a psychiatrist or counselor has recommended martial arts to help with attitude adjustments and learning disabilities. (Yes, it's great for that.)

We have had students that have actually gotten off their medication for Attention Deficit Disorder and even for depression after a few months' training.

Martial Arts Minute
The physical enhancements of Tae Kwon Do supersede any other activity or sport you may have participated in. You will lose weight, you will get in shape, and you won't even know you're doing it. You will be working every large muscle group of your body in a very natural way. Martial arts work with your body, not against it.

Watch Out, Grasshopper
Although the martial arts have many great psychical benefits, as with any form of strenuous exercise, you should consult with your physician before you start training if you have any questions.

Wise Sa Bum Tells Us
Most instructors suggest that parents wait until their kids are in first grade before signing them up for Tae Kwon Do. Some schools, however, have special programs for children as young as three or four. This is because it's never too early to begin building some physical coordination in little kids. Improved coordination will also help to develop their self-confidence at an early age.

Kids can gain self-confidence and discipline from Tae Kwon Do.

Presto, Change-O

Over the years I've tried to put into words how martial arts can actually change a person, and I've found it an almost impossible feat to accomplish. You'd pretty much have to experience it to understand why someone would want to study martial arts.

Most people think of Tae Kwon Do as an Olympic sport and a means of self-defense, while to the Tae Kwon Do expert, the ultimate goal is a perfection of self, involving things like inner peace and serenity. It also encompasses physical fitness thorough exercise, diet, and disciplined living. Finally, the martial artist strives to build his or her character based on timeless principles like *honor* and *loyalty*.

This seems like a strange paradox doesn't it? How can you achieve lofty goals like the perfection of mind, body, and spirit while learning how to snap kick some guy's testicles or poke his eyes out? Well, read on and be enlightened *Grasshopper*!

> **Martial Arts Minute**
> You will soon agree that the enhancement of the mental and physical self should be the main purpose of training.

When the Spirit Is Willing

Probably the most surprising enhancement that comes from martial arts training is the spiritual aspect. So you're not a spiritual person? Just wait. Martial arts have a way of making one spiritual. As a student you will be in awe of your environment and even of your own body. It will be an amazing discovery to know your body inside and out. You see how it can become a tool or an instant weapon if necessary.

A serious student of martial arts will soon become a serious student of life—always pondering this spiritual journey we call living. I'm not talking about religion here, I'm talking about your inner-most desires, your goals, and your attitude toward yourself and others. Ask any true practitioner and he'll tell you, martial arts isn't just an exercise program—it's a way of life. So why do we do the *Do*? We do it because it makes us complete—mentally, physically, and spiritually.

Never Pinch an Inch Again

I have already said that martial arts are a great way to get into shape but for those fitness buffs who think that Tae Kwon Do may not be enough of a workout for them, I encourage you to go and observe a class. As a former aerobics instructor and weight-trainer, I've found nothing more grueling and physically challenging than an hour's worth of martial arts training. There may not be as much bobbing and jogging as in an aerobics class, but there is constant body motion, and with each motion every ounce of power is utilized. For example, you don't just extend your arm, you punch with all the force that you can muster.

I can still remember the first day I signed up for lessons. I told my instructor that I was an aerobics instructor and was afraid that his class would not be enough *cardio* for me. My teacher didn't say anything back, he just smiled—a smile I learned to fear over the years.

You see, martial arts teaches the student how to use her body muscles naturally. You're not doing a lot of bulking-up, but your muscles will become toned by the natural flow of your body. Flexibility is also a natural element that will come with time. I am especially amused with some of the men who sign up, looking like they're made out of unbendable steel every time they try to stretch. But amazingly they are able to master full splits after a year or so of training.

You will sweat profusely, and like the beginning of any physical exercise, you will be sore for the first few

Watch Out, Grasshopper
If you have any specific needs or problems, like a bad back or weak knees, be sure to inform your instructor before you start. Always warm up before you begin a Tae Kwon Do workout. Because of the hard punches and high kicks, you could easily pull something if you aren't warmed up and ready for action.

weeks—usually in the knees, balls of the feet, and the lower back. The soreness will normally all fade in time as your muscles and joints adapt to the movements of kicking and punching—something they've never had to do before.

Tae Kwon Do will stretch you out.

Entering the Mental Gym

Some instructors like to point out that the martial arts are 90 percent mental. If you want to know what sets the martial artists apart from the weight trainers and aerobicisers, it's having to think about the execution of each and every move you do. You'll be sweating during your first few lessons from the mental concentration alone. Initially there's a lot to learn—seemingly more than you could learn in a lifetime—how to walk, how to stand, where to put your hands. Eventually it even gets to the point of holding your fingers correctly so you won't get injured when chopping or punching.

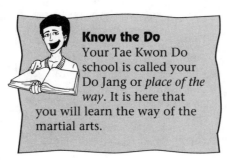

Know the Do
Your Tae Kwon Do school is called your Do Jang or *place of the way*. It is here that you will learn the way of the martial arts.

If you've ever wondered how Tae Kwon Do builds concentration, just imagine having to learn a whole new way of walking, talking, and moving your hands, and then putting all of these moves together so they flow with power and in unison. It's a whole new ball game, and like everything else in life, it simply has to be learned through practicing. Your arms and hands will be making movements that they've never had to make before, and this always gives way to human error. You'll accidentally hold your palm up instead of down; you'll straighten your elbows when they should be bent.

And if that isn't enough, you even have to learn how to breathe differently. On some moves you inhale, and on others you exhale. Breathing patterns go hand in hand with the execution of power.

Most Tae Kwon Do schools will start you off with some basic Korean terminology as well. You may feel a little dumb having to repeat everything your teacher says, but it's for a good reason. Most promotional examinations are conducted with many Korean words, and you'll have to get used to the language right away. It's all part of preserving the tradition.

Keeping the tradition also means being on your toes with the protocol. Learning when to answer back and when to keep quiet is something a weight trainer doesn't have to worry about with his coach. In martial arts timing is important, including when and when not to open your mouth. This too is all part of the mental training.

Teachers, Teachers, Everywhere!

Once you've decided you want to try Tae Kwon Do the hardest part starts. How do you find the right teacher? A quick check of the phone book will probably reveal a myriad of choices. We'll cover this topic in much greater detail in Chapter 5, "Finding the Right School," but let's just say here that there are as many different kinds of instructors as you might imagine.

Have you heard the old joke that asks, "What do they call the guy who graduated dead last in his medical school class?" Answer: "doctor." And Tae Kwon Do instructors don't have to have any kind of training even remotely similar to a graduate degree to hang up a shingle saying "Martial Arts Teacher."

The best advice we can give you here is to talk to prospective instructors and find one that is compatible not only with your needs but also with your personality.

> **Martial Arts Minute**
> Martial arts instructors do not judge you by your ability, but by your sincerity to learn.

The Least You Need to Know

> ➤ Tae Kwon Do is an *ageless* sport, you can be in nursery school or in your 70s.
> ➤ Tae Kwon Do is more than just *kicking butt*, it is the art of controlling your emotions.
> ➤ Tae Kwon Do really is a cardio workout; you will sweat and be sore, but greatly rewarded.
> ➤ Tae Kwon Do is a mental exercise. You will find that 90 percent of your workout will be mental because of the complete concentration that must go into even the simplest moves.

Digging Up the Roots of the Do

You may be wondering exactly what the difference is between Karate, Kung Fu, Tae Kwon Do, and all the other martial arts you've heard of. Karate, at least in the United States, is a very general term, much like the word *automobile*.

There are hundreds of different kinds of automobiles—Chevies, Fords, etc.—but each one is still considered an automobile. It's much the same thing with Karate.

Strictly speaking, Karate (literally *empty hand*) is a form of martial art originating in Okinawa around the 15th century and refined in Japan during the 20th century. Today, however, it has become a generic term referring to most of the *striking* schools of martial arts. There are many different *styles* of Karate today with names like Shotokan, Goju-Ryu, and Kenpo.

Know the Do

The martial arts can be divided into two broad categories, striking and grappling arts. *Striking* arts are (surprise) systems that favor kicks and punches. *Grappling* arts emphasize grabs, holds, and throws. Although many styles include techniques from both areas, most will fall mainly into one category or the other.

Martial Arts Minute

The monk Bodhidharma supposedly got sleepy during meditation himself, and one day to keep from dozing, he chopped off his own eyelids. That's one way to stay awake!

Another striking art you have probably heard of is Kung Fu (remember the old TV show?) Kung Fu (sometimes called Gung-Fu) originated in China and has even more different styles than Karate. Kung Fu literally means *well done* and in China applies to many other activities besides just martial arts. In fact, in mainland China, the term *wu-shu* is used for their system of martial arts. However, in Hong Kong (where all those Kung Fu movies are made) and in the rest of the world, Kung Fu has become a catch-all term for the Chinese arts. Bruce Lee and Jackie Chan are examples of famous Kung Fu practitioners.

Judo, Jujutsu, and Aikido are examples of *grappling* arts where you actually have to get your hands on the other guy by grabbing his limbs or clothes to do your stuff.

The Fighting Family Tree

Although fighting arts developed in most ancient cultures, the nations of the far East took the military, or martial, arts to a highly refined level. The roots of the Asian martial arts go back to the three most prevalent Asian nations...China, Japan, and Korea, where ancient soldiers and monks would study, among other things, the instinctive fighting habits of animals defending their own territory.

Legend has it that a monk named Bodhidharma devised the first system of martial training at the Shaolin Temple in China in the early 6th century. It seems the monks were prone to fall asleep during their many long hours of meditation, and Bodhidharma, who had previously studied some warrior methods in his native India, came up with a series of exercises to keep the sleepy monks a bit more alert and physically fit.

Table 2.1 Striking Arts vs. Grappling Arts

Striking Arts	Grappling Arts
Kung Ru (China)	Jujutsu/Judo (Japan)
Karate (Japan)	Aikido (Japan)
Tae Kwon Do (Korea)	Sumo (Japan)
Boxing (Europe/USA)	Wrestling (Europe/USA)

Trying to figure out if one kind of martial art is better than another is like comparing doctors. There are a lot of different kinds of doctors in the world, and they all have their own style of healing the sick. Which ones are good and which ones are not so good lies in the eyes of each individual patient. Apples to me, oranges to you. If someone is getting personal growth out of what they're studying, then it's good. By the same token, if someone is getting torn down mentally, physically, or spiritually by what they're studying, then it's not so good.

Three Kingdoms of Ancient Korea

Way back in the 6th century, the land that is now Korea consisted of three kingdoms: Silla, Paekche, and Korguryo. In Silla, the smallest of the three, there arose a warrior class known as the Hwarang or *flower of manhood*. Members were chosen from young sons of the nobility. These young men no doubt practiced the ancient Korean fighting system of Subak as well as studied weapons of war and esoteric subjects such as song and dance.

Know the Do
The Hwarang literally means *flower of manhood*. Boys as young as 12 were taken to learn cultural pursuits and military disciplines.

Guardian statues at ancient Korean temples have been found in martial arts poses.

Most historians say that the ancient fighting arts of not only Korea but also the other Asian nations were influenced by the Chinese systems springing out of Bodhidharma's exercises and being carried to all parts of the far East by traveling Buddhist monks. Others point out that since communication was so slow and sporadic in those days, the martial arts of Korea were only marginally influenced by the styles of China.

The three kingdoms of ancient Korea in the 6th century.

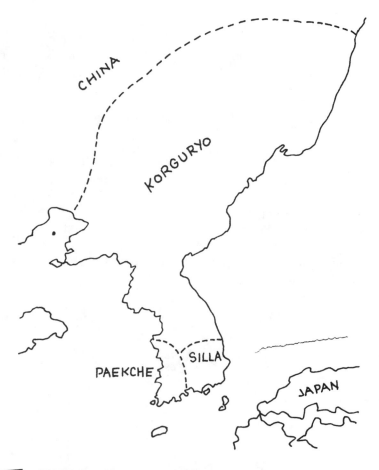

Several names for the ancient Korean fighting arts occur in old manuscripts, including Subak and Tae-Kyon, although historians do not know exactly what kind of techniques these arts utilized. Therefore the many modern Korean systems that claim to be almost exact duplicates of the ancient styles are stretching it a bit.

Following the Warrior Code

The Hwarang had a code of conduct similar to their neighboring warriors, the Japanese Samurai. The code of conduct of the Hwarang consisted of five main points:

➤ Loyalty to the king

➤ Obedience to parents

➤ Trust among friends

➤ Never retreat in battle

➤ Justice in killing

The strength of the Hwarang warriors was one of the main factors in the unification of the three kingdoms under Silla rule about 670 A.D. The Hwarang lasted through the Silla Dynasty and the following Koryo Dynasty (the modern name of Korea was derived from Koryo) until 1392 when the Yi Dynasty began. Unfortunately the warrior philosophy fell out of favor during these relatively peaceful times, and the fighting arts all but disappeared in the land.

From a drawing in the Moo Ye Dobo Tong Ji, *a record book of the ancient martial arts of Korea written in 1790.*

The Modern Era

Zooming all the way up to the early 20th century we find the Japanese army invading Korea in 1910. The Japanese tried, in essence, to wipe out the Korean culture. They outlawed the country's customs, including martial arts practice, and even changed the official language to Japanese. Try to imagine Russia invading America, giving everybody a Russian name, making everyone speak Russian, and outlawing football and everything on the FOX Network. Americans would be pretty upset. Well, the Koreans were too, but there wasn't anything they could do about it.

Many Koreans finally fled their homeland to try and find better conditions elsewhere. Some went to China and some, unbelievably, even to Japan itself. While in these other lands, some of these self-exiled Koreans began to practice the martial arts of China and Japan.

Know the Do
The Japanese Samurai had their own code of conduct known as *Bushido* or *way of the warrior*. The Japanese martial arts were known collectively as *Bujutsu* or *warrior arts*.

The end of World War II in 1945 finally freed the Koreans from Japanese oppression. New feelings of national pride and a desire to restore Korean customs led to the establishment of a number of new martial arts schools known as *kwans*. Here are a few that existed by 1949:

➤ Moo Duk Kwan—Institute (school) of Martial Virtue

➤ Ji Do Kwan—School of Wisdom

➤ Chang Moo Kwan—Martial Training School

➤ Chung Do Kwan—School of the Blue Wave

➤ Oh Do Kwan—School of My Way

Most kwans taught an eclectic blend of martial arts, part Chinese, part Japanese, and part indigenous Korean. In fact a commonly used name for their systems was *Tang Soo Do* or *way of the China hand*.

In 1955, the kwan's leaders decided on a new name that wouldn't reflect any other country except Korea. Tae Kwon Do, or *way of kicking and punching*, had been suggested by South Korean Army General Choi Hong Hi and was accepted as the moniker of the new unified Korean art. It can be spelled *Tae Kwon Do*, *Taekwondo*, or *Taekwan Do*. It's all the same thing. Some of the Korean instructors refused to accept the new name, however, and started their own systems separate from Tae Kwon Do. Some of these other modern Korean arts are:

➤ Hapkido—taught in many schools alongside Tae Kwon Do as a more self-defense–oriented and less a sport-oriented art

➤ Kuk Sool—a complicated style incorporating things like wrist locks and throws along with striking

➤ Hwarang-Do—similar to Kuk Sool and found much more extensively in the United States than in Korea itself

It's actually pretty amazing that in less than 50 years, the art of Tae Kwon Do has grown to over 30 million practitioners worldwide. And millions of them are in the United States (as you can tell by the number of Tae Kwon Do schools on practically every other corner in most big American cities).

Jhoon Rhee breaking bricks in a photo from the early 1960s.

Coming to the USA

In 1956 a young third-degree black belt named Jhoon Rhee arrived in San Marcos, Texas (near San Antonio) to introduce America to the Korean martial arts. At the time he still used the term Tang Soo Do, but in 1960 a visit by General Choi convinced him to use the new term Tae Kwon Do for the first time in the West. However, that term was used by Rhee and the other Koreans coming to this country in the 1950s and '60s as a kind of brand name to refer to what they still called their *Karate classes*. Americans, therefore, called themselves Karate practitioners even though they may have done Tae Kwon Do. As Jhoon Rhee said, "We didn't want the Americans to think we were an Oriental restaurant. They had at least heard of Karate."

In reality the Tae Kwon Do of the 1950s and '60s was very much like Japanese Karate. After all, the Korean masters had trained in Japan during the '30s and '40s during the Japanese occupation. General Choi was a second-degree black belt in Japanese Shotokan Karate and said in his first book that Tae Kwon Do was actually a mixture of Karate and Tae Kyon, one of the old indigenous systems of Korea.

Know the Do
We've mentioned Tang Soo Do as one of the earlier names for the Korean martial arts. Meaning *way of the China hand*, Tang Soo Do was the first translation of "Karate" in Japan. It was changed to *way of the empty hand* (different characters, same pronunciation) in an effort to make Karate more popular among the Japanese.

Many early Korean Karate champions went on to become famous in the emerging American martial arts world. Here Chuck Norris (left), as a Tang Doo Do stylist, and Skipper Mullins (right) mix it up in an early '60s tournament.

Many schools today use the terms Karate *and* Tae Kwon Do *interchangeably, because when the Koreans came to America in the 1950s and '60s, Karate was more recognizable than Tae Kwon Do.*

From Federations to the Olympics

Federations, associations, and styles can be important because they create a *brotherhood* or bond between fellow practitioners. Knowing that you have roots and belong to something larger than yourself helps build the strength and confidence necessary for creating, among other things, spirit. All martial artists take this bonding very seriously. Many have dedicated their entire lives to the cause of the preservation of the style or federation.

This attitude of brotherhood is something instructors will start building right away in even the youngest of students. It is often explained this way: We've all fought with our brothers and sisters at home, but should someone ever threaten our siblings at school, we are always the first to run to their defense. It's the same way in the martial arts. Internal matters between ourselves may get ugly, but we'll always stick together.

This kind of unity was what was in the mind of the Republic of South Korea when, in 1961, General Choi was elected president of the first official Tae Kwon Do organization, the Korean Tae Kwon Do Association. Unfortunately he was soon forced out by his political rivals (an example of one of those ugly internal squabbles). In 1966 Choi left South Korea and formed the International TKD Federation in Canada. To fill the void in South Korea, the World TKD Federation was established in 1973 by Dr. Kim Un-young.

Today we've got both the ITF and the WTF as well as several other large organizations (see Appendix A, "Associations and Federations,"). The ITF makes claims to be the *official* federation for Tae Kwon Do since it was first. Likewise the WTF says they are the *official* Tae Kwon Do organization because they have the support of the South Korean government, and they have their world headquarters at the Kukkiwon in Seoul, South Korea.

The WTF has been recognized by the International Olympic Committee, and Tae Kwon Do became a demonstration sport at the 1988 Olympics, an exhibition sport in the 1992 Olympics, and gains full medal status as an Olympic sport in the year 2000.

Other organizations have tried to be so recognized, but right now the WTF is the only group holding Olympic-style competitions. The WTF has, in fact, changed the emphasis of Tae Kwon Do since it's founding in 1973. The WTF style has become less Karate-like by stressing high kicks and reducing the role of punching. Not all Tae Kwon Do schools have taken kindly to the changes, but it has been hard to argue with the success of getting into the Olympics.

Martial Arts Minute
Many world-famous Tae Kwon Do masters have their own associations, and you can see why some people can't figure out which organization is which. Suffice it to say, it matters less which group your instructor belongs to than his or her ability to teach you well.

Co-author Keith Yates demonstrates a flying side kick in this mid-1980s photo. He is the founder of one of those other associations, the American Karate and Tae Kwon Do Organization (A-KaTo).

Modern Do Philosophy

Though the politics of Tae Kwon Do continue to be a sticking point with many practitioners, the basic ethics of the art remain the same and can be agreed on by all. One long-standing philosophy is that no matter what your convictions are, the important thing is that you do everything 100 percent from your heart.

The word *do* means *way* and implies more than just a method. In most martial arts (like Judo, Aikido, Karate, and even Tae Kwon Do), it refers more to a path, as in a path you take in life. Though the politics of Tae Kwon Do many continue to change, as politics inevitably will, the basic principles have and will remain the same.

All traditional martial arts set the same goals before us. Two very important ones are:

➤ To achieve harmony with nature and yourself

➤ To gain balance by controlling both the positive and the negative forces in your life (Um vs. Yang, or in Chinese, Yin Yang)

Wise Sa Bum Tells Us

The Yin Yang symbol represents the interflow of two opposing forces. According to Asian philosophy, all life is composed of a balance between forces like light and darkness, male and female, war and peace, etc.

The Yin Yang.

Knowing the Creed

Many Tae Kwon Do schools have a kind of student creed that is repeated at the end of every class. The teacher will ask, "How do we build self-confidence?" The students answer, "Through knowledge in the mind, honesty in the heart, and strength in the body." The instructor should make sure the students understand the meaning behind the pledge.

Self-confidence starts with knowledge. Knowledge is important because it teaches you what is valuable to you. If you offer a monkey a banana or a diamond, which will he take? The banana, of course. The monkey doesn't know the diamond is more valuable. As a student of Tae Kwon Do and of life, you should concentrate just as much on work (or on school work) as you do on your art. If you can learn your martial arts techniques, you can learn your job or your school lessons. Parents love it when the instructor stresses school work to the kids in class.

But you cannot stop with simple knowledge. There are a lot of smart people who don't use their brains for good purposes. Some criminals are pretty smart. You must also be a good person inside. You must have a good heart to use your knowledge wisely. You must be honest. What is honesty? Not lying. Do people like you when you lie? Do you like yourself when you lie? So by being honest and by not lying, not only are you doing the right thing, but you will like yourself better and other people will also like you.

The last thing is action. What good is knowledge if you don't act on that knowledge? Because you must have the strength to back your knowledge with action, you must exercise every day. Eat correctly every day. Practice your Tae Kwon Do every day. When you have done all this, your body will be strong. This is the message of Tae Kwon Do. A true martial artist embodies a perfect balance of intellect, emotional character, and strength, or *mind-body-spirit.*

23

Learning the Tenets

Many Tae Kwon Do schools post a list of *tenets* to be used as a guide for the moral development of a student:

➤ Courtesy

➤ Humility

➤ Integrity

➤ Perseverance

➤ Self-control

➤ Indomitable spirit

Courtesy is demonstrating respect and consideration for others. Humility is not thinking of yourself more highly than you should. Integrity is keeping your promises and being trustworthy in the eyes of others. Perseverance is always striving to do your best. Self-control is maintaining your temper and staying calm in the face of a stressful situation. The last tenet, indomitable spirit, is similar to perseverance but instead of being expressed in a positive way (always strive), indomitable spirit is represented by a negative—never, never, never give up. It's kind of the Winston Churchill tenet.

Martial Arts Minute
One way to remember the tenets of Tae Kwon Do is to memorize the phrase, *eat your CHIPS with Indomitable Spirit.* Get it? C-H-I-P-S-I. Some school list the tenets in a slightly different order. Others may translate them a little differently (like modestly instead of humility).

Finally there are further stated objectives for the students in many schools that include these promises:

➤ To develop an appreciation for Tae Kwon Do as a sport and as an art

➤ To achieve physical fitness through positive participation

➤ To improve mental discipline and emotional control

➤ To learn self-defense skills

➤ To develop a sense of responsibility for oneself and others

Hey, It's Not a Religion

Tae Kwon Do, like many martial arts, has Asian roots that some associate with religious principles and precepts. However no religion is ever stressed or impressed upon students who study Tae Kwon Do. In fact, if it is important to you, the well-respected Christian Research Foundation did a study on the martial arts and found Tae Kwon Do to be the art with the least amount of Buddhist or Confucian influence. Indeed, the Tae Kwon Do principles that we have outlined above transcend any one religion, and no one can argue with their importance for daily life and practice for everyone.

The Least You Need to Know

- ➤ Tae Kwon Do is one of the *striking* schools of the martial arts where Jujutsu and Aikido are *grappling*.
- ➤ The ancient Korean Hwarang warriors had a code of conduct; it was a guide for their everyday life.
- ➤ After World War II many martial arts schools sprang up in Korea because of the desire to re-establish Korean culture.
- ➤ The Korean martial arts came to America in 1956.
- ➤ There are several large Tae Kwon Do associations in the United States and the world.
- ➤ Tae Kwon Do is more than a physical activity as seen in its various creeds and tenets outlining moral and ethical standards.
- ➤ You should find the best instructor with the best philosophy for yourself regardless of affiliation.

Chapter 3

The Most Important Muscle: The One Between Your Ears

In This Chapter

➤ Discovering the role your attitude plays in your training

➤ Finding out how Tae Kwon Do can build self-confidence

➤ Understanding why Bruce Lee screamed so much

➤ Learning how your training will get you in touch with your body

➤ Focusing on the task at hand through meditation

I cracked open a fortune cookie not long ago and it read: "One must first learn to obey before he can command." I wouldn't have thought a fortune cookie would end up in this book, but this statement is perfect for epitomizing the traditional martial arts attitude. Someone has said that success is mental. Your mental attitude comes from your brain, the most important muscle you'll utilize in Tae Kwon Do (okay, I know it's not technically a muscle, but I'll bet you'll remember this principle now). Attitude is everything. I've seen students fail their black belt test, some more than once, because of their attitude.

Humble Pie

One of the tenets of Tae Kwon Do is humility. And, let's face it, when you can kick most people's rear ends it is sometimes hard to be humble. But this is a very important element of your martial arts character. A martial artist is expected to be strong and confident, yet gracious and humble.

I often tell students to think of it this way: Let's say there are two college football players that are both equally outstanding at what they do. One of these players is known for having a good attitude and doesn't brag about his accomplishments. The other player is known for letting his ability go to his head. He is boastful and arrogant. He might even break the law and then expect that no one will care because he is a famous athlete. Finally draft day comes and both players get the chance to turn pro. Which one of these men is most likely to get picked? Everyone may love a winner, but not everyone will support a winner with a bad attitude.

> **Watch Out, Grasshopper**
>
> Keeping a good attitude includes not losing your temper while sparring, even if someone kicks you where it hurts. Striking back when accidentally, or even purposefully, hit is a sure sign of a lack of self-control!

In Tae Kwon Do, the higher you climb in rank, the more humble you are expected to become. So, if you run into a Grandmaster, which is the highest achievable position in the art, you should find yourself facing a very humble individual. Of course people are people, and not everyone is going to be this way, but Korean masters highly frown upon someone of high-ranking with a "big head." Since there is always someone with a higher rank than you, there is an unwritten system of checks and balances to make sure everybody stays *out of the clouds*, so to speak.

Being humble is not just for the classroom either. You are expected to be a gracious winner in the ring and in life. There's something to be said about maintaining a balanced perspective about the events in your life, whether good or bad. In my own organization, students are not awarded their black belts until months after they've tested. Our Grandmaster has chosen to do this purposely so that students will not be overly excited about this new step in their life. Humility leads to a calm attitude toward everything.

> **Martial Arts Minute**
>
> Humility can be seen in the kind of respect you show those in authority. For example, don't walk through a door in front of a higher-ranked black belt. Contrary to our Western rules of etiquette, even women students should step back and let the male instructor walk through the door first. This shows humility on your part.

Even in fighting competitions, you must to learn how to calm down before you can become a good fighter. If you are overly excited, you will miss blocking the many kicks and punches that will come your way, ultimately causing you to lose the match. This parallels your life. Learning not to get too excited but to remain calm about all the *attacks* that come your way in the everyday world helps keep your life in balance.

Patience Please

Another important aspect of having a good martial arts attitude is patience. Before you can have patience with others, you first have to master being patient with yourself. This is a hard one. I see the absence of this particular aspect every time a student experiences a sense of disappointment when he or she can't get a move down. Often I've felt like stopping the lesson and saying, "Okay, if you want to kick yourself in the butt, do it now so that we can continue."

If you've ever had the idea that you can just jump in and do whatever it is you want to do perfectly, your first few Tae Kwon Do lessons will halt this idea immediately. When it comes to the martial arts, you'll learn to be patient with yourself, or you won't be able to continue with your training simply because you'll become frustrated.

Once you've learned how to be patient and to live with yourself, faults and all, you can then extend this courtesy to others around you. More than likely, no one in class will ever condemn you for not being able to perform a certain move because they themselves have been there. Unless you laugh at yourself for doing something wrong, no one in class will laugh at you. We learn to forgive others for their shortcomings because we have learned how to forgive ourselves for our own lack of perfection.

A Can-Do Do Attitude

Tae Kwon Do, like all other martial arts, works best when it's working in your mind. Another important key to success is self-confidence. When you finally believe in yourself, your whole world can change because you begin to feel like you have enough inner-strength to conquer your greatest fears.

As someone who's always had a fear of deep water, I can personally testify to this concept. As a child I almost drowned in a swimming pool. Even after swimming lessons, my mind would not let me grasp the fact that we all have a buoyancy rate. One day while sitting around the pool, I realized that I had accomplished some incredible feats as a martial artist. The fact that I had made it all the way to black belt was a milestone in itself. So why was it that I could not accomplish something as natural as swimming, something that the smallest of children near me seemed to have no fear of doing?

Wise Sa Bum Tells Us

A handshake that isn't firm shows a lack of self-confidence!

That day changed my life. I got up, walked over to the deep end of the pool, and I jumped in. (Do not try this at home unless you know how to swim. I had taken swimming lessons before.) I obviously got the hang of it, because here I am today telling the story.

Once you begin to believe in yourself, it also becomes more difficult to believe some of the things that would normally upset you. For instance, if I tried to insult you and said that you are the most polka-dotted person I've ever seen, you would go away laughing. It's very obvious that you're not polka-dotted, and you know that as a fact. However, if I were to say that your are the most ridiculous person I've ever seen, you would become offended. Why? Because you don't believe, 100 percent, that you are not ridiculous in some way. We can only be offended when something comes a little too close for comfort.

Discipline

From the well of self-confidence will flow self-control and discipline. Aristotle said that discipline is doing something you don't want to in order to achieve the greater good. Tae Kwon Do training can be fun, but it can also be so hard that sometimes you just don't want to do it. The sweat, the effort, the bruises—sometimes you would rather stay home. But you've got to have the discipline to get down to the Do Jang. You do it because you are gaining something greater.

The more you train, the more you will believe in yourself. Once you've grasped how hard work and dedication can get you results, it's very easy to apply this same concept to the other areas of your life. The discipline needed to stop bad habits, for instance, does not seem as difficult once you've discovered how the game plan works. If you can accomplish some of the feats that you have within your own training, then you can eventually accomplish anything that you put your mind to. If you think this way, you will start to feel it within just a few months of training.

It takes discipline to eat right. It takes discipline to exercise regularly. It takes discipline to say no to habits that are detrimental to our bodies. I'm not saying that studying Tae Kwon Do and other martial arts is the cure-all to the world's every problem, but it's a start.

Wise Sa Bum Tells Us

Discipline can be seen in the simple act of just standing or sitting still during instruction time in class. This can be particularly difficult for little kids (and even for some of us big kids!).

Inner Spirit

Another development in your training will be the cultivation of your inner spirit. Most people aren't even aware of this aspect in their lives today, but the Asian society has been aware of the spiritual application since the very conception of martial arts, even coining the phrase "body, mind, and spirit." I'm not talking about the time you were an altar boy when you were 12 years old, but about what sits at the very center of a man and makes him tick.

Of body, mind, and spirit, the most important is the spirit. If you think about it, some day our bodies will be too old to kick high and punch hard. Our minds may even grow dull, causing us to become forgetful. But our spirit will always remain. Even after death, it remains in the hearts of those we have left behind.

During our lifetime, we may spend countless hours in the gym developing our bodies. We also spend time and money educating ourselves to develop our minds, yet what have we done to develop our spiritual sense? Tae Kwon Do, just like many other martial arts, can be and should be about spiritual enhancement. Once a student discovers this aspect within himself, he will then begin to feel the completeness of becoming a balanced individual.

What's All the Screaming About?

In Korean the word for the Tae Kwon Do yell is "ki ahp." It literally means *spirit shout*. When people are really scared, they scream (yes, even men). Screaming is a natural response of the inner spirit. So the scream of a martial artist is an amplification of the spirit.

Just like soldiers yell when they charge up the hill, the scream shows that you are confident and ready. I can always tell the confidence a student has in themselves and in their technique by their ki ahp. Just as an intruder is discouraged by the loud barking of a dog, an opponent is discouraged when someone is constantly screaming at him. That's why the martial artist is always screaming (have you ever seen a Bruce Lee movie?).

Wise Sa Bum Tells Us

The Tae Kwon Do yell comes from deep from within, both literally and figuratively. Don't puff out your cheeks and scream from your throat. Call up the air from your diaphragm, like an opera singer, and belt out a low-sounding, fearsome *spirit shout*.

We've all seen the TV sitcoms where someone has happened upon a "ku-rutty" expert, and they hear all those "hi-yahs!" and other strange sounds. Even watching those Bruce Lee movies can make you want to grab the earplugs at times. But there really is something to all the screaming.

Think of the times you've picked up something heavy, an over-stuffed garbage can, for example. You probably grunted or even yelled out at the same time you were picking it up. Getting vocal not only deadens the pain in your arms or back, but it also gives you an extra boost of power.

*A loud yell gives
you more power.*

If you don't believe me, then I invite you to come watch the board-breaking portion of a promotional test at my school. Those who don't scream when making contact with the board rarely break it board. But even the smallest of children, weighing no more than 50 pounds, can bust through a pine board when they learn how to vocalize and direct their power.

> **Know the Do**
> *Jip Joong* means concentration. *Jiptjung* is the concept of power gathering, or breathing at the point of blocking or striking to unify the internal and external powers.

Yes, Tae Kwon Do classes can get very noisy at times, and not all screams are the same, but no scream is ever incorrect. So when should a student scream? In forms (practice routines), the scream is already choreographed into the pattern. In fighting, you'll discover when a scream is necessary by getting a feel for when you need that extra boost of power. It is usually on every kick and punch intended to score. But when in doubt, I always tell my students, just scream.

Honor Thy Master and Thyself

Having respect is a lot like having patience, in that before you can respect others, you must first respect yourself. Tae Kwon Do teaches respect for yourself and for others in many different ways.

You develop respect for yourself by simply discovering what an incredible tool your body is. Your training will introduce you to your body in ways you never thought possible. You begin to see what a tremendous weapon it can instantly become. You start to know what your physical strong points are, as well as your limitations.

When I began to know my body inside and out, I developed such a high respect for myself that I chose to no longer participate in things that I felt were unhealthy. My body is a fantastic machine; I've seen it in action. Why would I ever want to poison it with tobacco, alcohol, or anything else?

Upon making such great discoveries about your body and ultimately about yourself, you will feel a great sense of gratitude toward your instructor. This is the person who has helped you find yourself and has made you who you are today. To say that you will respect this person is an understatement. At times you will feel like you owe him or her your life. A good instructor will command respect not by constantly yelling at you, but by a rare combination of skills and character. You'll want to be like him. You'll want to follow him.

> **Watch Out, Grasshopper**
> Respect means taking instruction even if you don't agree. Arguing back when being corrected ("My leg IS straight!") is considered very disrespectful.

> **Wise Sa Bum Tells Us**
> Out of respect, a student will bow out before fighting his instructor in a competition.

And Now, a Moment of Silence

Meditation is misunderstood by a lot of Westerners. Some people think of it as religious. It's true that many religions (from Buddhists to Christians) practice meditation, but the act of meditation is not, by itself, religious.

In the martial arts, meditation is often used to help students focus on the task at hand. And your task in a Tae Kwon Do class is not to worry about a bad day at school or the office. Your task is not to worry about how you'll look to the other students in class or if you'll make a fool of yourself. Your task is merely to try your best, to learn something, to better yourself.

Martial Arts Minute
Kneeling or sitting mediation before or after practice is common. It clears your mind and prepares you for the next stage, either a hard workout or re-entry into the world outside the Do Jang. In this posture you must sit straight up and breathe evenly and deeply. This can last from a few seconds to minutes. Some masters meditate for an hour a day.

Preparation in meditation can help the student forget about what he or she is not supposed to be concentrating on and instead focus totally on the psychical (and mental) activity at hand. This relaxed but focused state that you'll learn to develop in the martial arts can and will help you in many other areas of life as well.

Children can be a different story. Many are too young to grasp this process of earning mutual respect, so respect is demanded from day one. Believe me when I tell you that children want to be told what to do. In martial arts, you give them a set of rules to play by. If they play by these rules, they are rewarded; if they don't, they are reprimanded. You can't argue with it; it's a system that's worked for hundreds of years (and not just in the martial arts either). I've seen this system turn out some pretty incredible kids—kids who respect not only themselves but others.

Mediation is often used to get you in the right frame of mind.

Respect has been part of the Tae Kwon Do tradition from the very start. Keeping traditions is considered sacred among many practitioners. To be honest, I myself do not fully understand all of these traditions, but they are our roots. Cut the roots off of a plant and you've got yourself a dead plant.

The Least You Need to Know

➤ Confidence and humility go hand in hand.

➤ Being well-balanced includes training the body, mind, and spirit.

➤ Screaming can give you an energy boost.

➤ The first step to having respect for others is to respect yourself.

➤ Martial arts meditation isn't a religious practice, but is a way to help you concentrate on your training.

Chapter 4

Why Tae Kwon Do Beats Little League, Soaps, and Bingo

In This Chapter

➤ Discovering how Tae Kwon Do can change a child's attitude and outlook on life

➤ Being a female martial artist and still maintaining your femininity

➤ Keeping you younger and healthier

➤ Having a physical limitation is no excuse for not taking Tae Kwon Do

I have already pointed out that the majority of Tae Kwon Do students these days are kids. Maybe that's because the experts are agreeing that the martial arts are a great activity for children. Why would an ancient Asian artform be so beneficial for modern Western kids raised on rock 'n' roll and television? Think about it for a minute. What do we seem to admire about Asian society: respect for elders; commitment to hard work and quality; loyalty to bosses and to family. These are things that many parents wish would rub off on our kids. And what better way to do that than signing the little tykes up for something that they love doing anyway?

I am also sold on the benefits of Tae Kwon Do for women. As a female practitioner, I can honestly say that the martial arts experience has changed my life. In the Do Jang, women are not second-class citizens. Everybody, regardless of gender, can accomplish as much as they can dream.

And what if you think you're too old to take up something like Tae Kwon Do? Well, my friend, I have news for you. Nothing could be farther from the truth. Do Jangs across the country and around the world are filled with students over 40 and even over 50 or 60. It's a great way to stay young.

Tae Kwon Do for the Hyperactive Child

Does your child, or some child you know, have trouble staying in one place for longer than a few seconds? Public schools around the country are plagued with the problem of hyperactive kids. In fact, some studies suggest that almost a third of the children in schools are on some kind of medication for this problem. I've had many young students who can't seem to concentrate on anything without their daily dosage. But I have noticed a dramatic improvement even after a few lessons in the Do Jang. I don't know if it is the desire to keep up with the other kids in class or if it's because I stress the importance of staying still and listening, but soon these little jumping beans are standing at attention and yelling, "yes, ma'am" or "yes, sir."

Special Education for Special Kids

Psychologists and therapists across the country also highly recommend martial arts for young patients with learning or behavior problems. Why? Because of the highly disciplined structure and overall learning environment a good Tae Kwon Do teacher can offer.

Knowledge in the mind…

Honesty in the heart...

Strength in the body.

Misbehavior is dealt with by knuckle push-ups and sometimes by a *time out* on the sidelines. Some kids may not mind missing a half an hour of math class sitting in the principal's office, but if they miss some Tae Kwon Do time, they may not be able to take the next belt promotion. It's a great motivation to behave.

Wise Sa Bum Tells Us

If your child has any kind of learning problem or physical difficulty, be sure and explain the situation fully to the instructor. Often they will have some great suggestions that will help your child both inside and outside the Do Jang.

This same principle works with children who may have a learning disability. Psychologists say that if certain kids find an activity that they really enjoy and want to participate in, they will make an unusual effort to stay focused. This ability gradually seeps over into other areas of learning.

Now I am not saying that the martial arts are a cure-all for every kind of problem that children might have, but I do know that I have seen near miraculous transformations with kids that many others have given up on.

"Oh No, Not Johnny!"

Let's face it, some kids just are a little slow at developing physical coordination. These are the poor little girls and boys who get picked last in P.E. team games. "I guess we'll take Johnny, he's the last one left," doesn't do much for Johnny's self-confidence.

But unlike volleyball or basketball, Tae Kwon Do is an individual sport where everyone can go at his or her own pace. If a child has trouble with a certain technique, he isn't letting the whole team down. That's why so many kids have bad experiences in team sports and give them up only to be deprived of all the advantages of physical activity.

Yes, football, soccer, baseball, and basketball are all great American pastimes that can teach children things like the value of hard work, sportsmanship, and teamwork. But there is simply no other physical activity like martial arts that can provide as much *internal* and individual character training. Tae Kwon Do teaches self-respect, self-commitment, self-esteem, self-discipline, and self-control.

The beauty of Tae Kwon Do is you don't have to be an overly athletic kid to be good at it. Everyone who starts pretty much stinks at first. Children who train in any type of martial arts can and will become outstanding students under only one condition—that they stick with it! Soon kids develop a great sense of respect for themselves as they start to see the improvements and incredible feats that can be accomplished through a little hard work and determination. You should see the faces of kids who break their first board or flip their first opponent.

Tae Kwon Do is known for its individual pace and skill levels—and its high kicks!

Any kid can do the Do.

Young people can learn self-discipline through Tae Kwon Do training and competition.

This is how martial arts build confidence in children. A kid who learns to respect himself or herself in the Do Jang will also be encouraged to try other difficult things in life. That's because he already understands how the pattern of success has worked through his Tae Kwon Do training.

From Fs to As?

Believe it or not, many students who do poorly in academic subjects have actually greatly improved after just a few months of martial arts. In my own school, I've seen a 180-degree turnaround in many of these kids. Straight F students have become A, B honor-roll students. Juvenile delinquents turn respectable, and those who just can't seem to listen to Mom and Dad will soon discover why and how they should listen. Often the instructor will request to see report cards and will periodically meet with Mom and Dad to see how things are going at home. Most schools set up some kind of merit system with the children resulting in praise and sometimes special rewards like certificates or patches when improvement is seen in school work. If a bad report is given, nothing hurts a kid more than seeing his respected instructor disappointed.

Wise Sa Bum Tells Us

Many Tae Kwon Do schools reward students for good academic marks with a patch or certificate. Sometimes recognition from the Sa Bum is more important to a child than parental approval.

Not to Worry

Probably the three most common questions asked by parents are: at what age should a child start taking lessons, will he or she get hurt, and will we have a problem with little Johnny hauling off and beating the living crap out of everybody else at school?

Most instructors will not take a youngster under the age of five or six, and there's a good reason for that. Motor skills necessary for martial arts are usually not developed until about that age. Though there are kids who will develop these skills earlier, most will become frustrated if allowed to take lessons before they can do the basic moves. If you have a question about whether or not your child is ready for Tae Kwon Do, ask an instructor to take your child out on the floor for a few minutes. At that time it will become very obvious to all whether or not he or she is ready to sign up. Sometimes waiting just six more months can make all the difference in the world. Flip over to Chapter 5, "Finding the Right School," on finding a good school for a little more on this topic.

As far as injury rates go, don't worry. Less than 1 percent of children will sustain any kind of injury because of martial arts training. Most other sports could never make that claim! Yes, your kids are learning fighting and self-defense, but they are also learning self-control and proper distancing. If you have any doubts, you can check out the school first by observing the children's class. You should always be able to walk away from class with a good feeling.

Wise Sa Bum Tells Us

While children are told to never show off, sometimes they can't resist the urge. If your find out your kid has been doing inappropriate Tae Kwon Do *lessons* at school, let the instructor know. He or she will deal with it quickly.

Finally, children are taught from day one that their Tae Kwon Do skills really do work. They are never to use them unless they are physically threatened. This means that they will learn how to deal with name-calling and even walk away from a potential fighting situation. When someone physically grabs or attempts to hit them, then, and only then, are they allowed to defend themselves with their Tae Kwon Do. Furthermore, monkeying around with martial arts techniques is definitely not acceptable behavior. A good school will instill this in a child right away. I have found that there is little danger that a young martial arts student will attempt to use or even to show off his or her skills.

For example, in our Do Jang we have several kids who have signed up for Tae Kwon Do lessons because of getting picked on at the local school bus stop. Although they now have the ability to defend themselves, getting picked on doesn't seem to bother them anymore. Kids who come to our classes because of the bus stop thing usually resolve this dilemma all by themselves simply because they gain enough confidence to make it go away.

Women Who Do the Do

There was a time in the martial arts (not only in Asia but also in this country) when the very thought of a woman practicing the warrior systems was out of the question. But today more women are doing the Do than ever before. At my own school, the women will outnumber the men in attendance in many classes.

Author Karen Eden demonstrates her form.

Speaking as a female I can honestly say that the martial arts have changed my life. How? Let me explain. Women are brought into this world and dressed in pink. Your brother gets a cap gun while you get a cuddly doll. A girl is raised to be soft and pretty, while a boy is raised to be brave and strong. Unless a series of events leads a girl to believe otherwise, she will grow up feeling more vulnerable, usually expecting the opposite sex to run to her defense when necessary. And we're not even touching on the times she'll go through life feeling like a total victim!

Don't get me wrong. There is nothing wrong with a girl being soft and pretty, I strive to be this way every day. But what's wrong with a girl being brave and strong as well? Tae Kwon Do can change a girl's life by teaching her how to utilize her own confidence for strength and bravery. And should there be any question, she will definitely know that she was *not* brought into this world to be victimized!

> **Martial Arts Minute**
> Arlene Limas won a gold medal in the first Tae Kwon Do competition in the Olympics. She started as a Kung Fu stylist and won many American open-style tournaments. When Tae Kwon Do was accepted as an Olympic sport in 1990, she switched styles and began training in Tae Kwon Do rules. Arlene is a prime example of a female martial arts champion.

I Could, I Wood

My favorite part of a promotional test is watching the face of a woman who will have to break a board for the first time in her life. Not knowing if she can actually pull this off, apprehension soon turns to disbelief once she puts her hand through that first piece of pine wood. Believe me, nothing will ever be the same. After that, you just know there's nothing you can't do once you put your mind to it. I've seen women go from being intimidated with little self-respect to feeling absolutely invincible in every part of their life because of their Karate training.

Do Jang Equality

While there is mutual respect for gender, women are not *cut a break* when it comes to Tae Kwon Do. They are expected to fight as hard, sweat as hard, and do just as many knuckle push-ups as their male counterparts. Though I didn't feel this way initially, this is one aspect of my training that I really began to appreciate. Being treated equally regardless of one's sex, even when it comes to the physical element, proves to the female practitioner that she can do something she's always been told was impossible: she can keep up with *the boys*.

Wise Sa Bum Tells Us

Women tend to be a little more limber than men but weaker as far as muscular strength goes. Work on your weaknesses. Moderate weight lifting will not build big, bulky muscles but will increase your strength and endurance.

Simply put, martial arts don't show favoritism to size or gender. Effective techniques can be utilized from the smallest to the largest of bodies. Of course basic biology deems that women do not have the same amount of muscle mass as men or, in most cases, the same reach. But since effective technique has little to do with muscle mass or the length of one's arms and legs, women are encouraged to hold their own against the opposite sex in fighting situations during class. A skilled female practitioner can offset the advantage that a male might have by using her skill instead of her strength.

After an amazingly short period of time, fighting with men is no big deal. Besides, in a real, life-threatening situation, it's almost always a man that a woman will have to defend herself against. You might as well get used to it in a controlled situation.

Challenges and Concerns of the Female Warrior

I've always said that, if given the choice, I'd rather fight a man than a woman. I don't know if we women are out to prove ourselves, or if we're just oblivious to pain, but female fighters can be brutal! Part of it is that *never say die* attitude that I find so impressive in the women who have made it all the way to the black belt level. You have to understand, it's not so much that these women are outstanding martial artists (and they are), but that they have mastered the skill of self-discipline. If asked, most would probably tell you that they are where they are simply because they never gave up. And believe me, there are plenty of times that a woman would want to throw in the towel during martial arts training.

The traditional martial arts uniform is probably the first frustration. It's not exactly engineered to fit a woman's body. It seems to be too loose where it needs to fit tighter and too tight where it needs to be more loose. Like other martial arts, Tae Kwon Do used to be predominately male-oriented. Those days are over, but you wouldn't know it by the amount of dressing room space women are sometimes allotted. Imagine trying to don this awkward-fitting uniform while getting elbowed and stepped on by other women!

Women can fight just as effectively as men.

Tae Kwon Do is an equal opportunity sport.

Perhaps the biggest challenge a female student faces is the mental aspect. You can't think of yourself as a *woman*, you have to think of yourself as a *student*. In class, you should only be known for your rank. However, this is not always the case for women. There have been many times in my career when, even as a black belt and instructor, male students would not give me the respect I had worked so hard to achieve. Some wouldn't bow, and some just couldn't find it in themselves to refer to me as "ma'am." I used to find this very frustrating and would retaliate by teaching them an extra difficult lesson. But now I've learned to let it go, realizing that these men have a problem with their own security and usually, with time, they do come around.

There are also those who refuse to give a female martial artist respect because they feel that they can physically conquer them. They think there's nothing a woman could ever teach them. Whether or not you can beat up a female is not the point. As a female instructor, I have something that most students aspire to get, a black belt. If nothing else, I can pass my knowledge on to others so that they too can become a black belt someday. That alone is enough to earn me respect.

Wise Sa Bum Tells Us

Pregnant women need not feel that they must stop their training. I know many who have trained up to their date of delivery, and every one of these women say it was the easiest delivery they've ever experienced. As far as changes in your training during this time, it's a good idea to avoid any type of sparring since accidental hits can happen. And go at a slower pace if you feel the need. However most of the pregnant women I have taught have said that they never felt the need to do so.

Doing the Do Over 45

Martial arts are truly ageless sports. If you're like me, hearing about washed-up Olympians at 30 sounds pretty scary. That's something a Tae Kwon Do practitioner will never have to worry about. So much of your success depends on efficiency of movement and proper technique that strength and speed (things that diminish with age) becomes less and less of a factor. This is why you can frequently see older martial artists out-scoring much younger opponents on the mat.

Don't think that you will stick out like a sore thumb if you have a little gray in your hair. Everyone in class will greatly respect your efforts. A lot of this stems from the Asian beliefs about growing older.

In Korea, Japan, and China it is considered an honor to grow old. The elderly are treated with such respect that people actually look forward to growing old! It is their belief that infinite wisdom comes with age and a crown of gray hair. Certainly the physical body will deteriorate, but the experiences of life that an older person has endured makes him or her such a valuable member of society.

This philosophy is still seen in traditional Tae Kwon Do schools today. The original Masters and Grandmasters who are still around, though they no longer have the physical skills that they once had, are still held in highest regard.

So you're over 45 and you haven't done a thing since 10th-grade gym class? Yes, you can still do Tae Kwon Do. No, you don't have to wait until you're in better shape and you've lost a few pounds. Come as you are; your body will naturally make the adjustments necessary, when it's necessary.

Martial Arts Minute
Jhoon Rhee, the acknowledged *Father of American Tae Kwon Do*, does 1,000 push-ups a day at the age of 65. He can do 100 push-ups in 60 seconds flat. One of his favorite sayings is, "the mind of a 100-year-old in the body of a 20-year-old."

Doing the Do over 45.

Most people over 45 who are considering Tae Kwon Do have concerns about not being able to keep up in class. You will be encouraged to go at your own pace. Also, no one is expecting you to kick over your head like a 16-year-old student. In the martial arts, you work with what God gave you.

Many a black belt has been issued for those who take a daily dose of Geritol. One particular new recruit from my school was 72 years old. Okay, Bruce Lee she wasn't, but she was doing something to change her life. She looked forward to every single lesson, and she could kick you hard enough in the shin to make every single step you climbed the next day feel like you were climbing Mt. Everest!

There are even advantages to starting your training over 45. One is having the patience to go all the way with your training. This is something that the average 21-year-old struggles with on a daily basis. Also the physical advantages benefiting the older student are absolutely incredible. Staying fit and active has been proven to reverse the effects of aging. At 57, my own instructor has amazed me with his tremendous strength and flexibility, as well as his youthful vigor. Those who train in martial arts such as Tae Kwon Do swear by it, saying that it keeps them young and healthy.

Watch Out, Grasshopper

Older students have to warm up a little longer than the kids or risk muscle strain. You might try to get to class early to stretch before the official bow-in.

Basics are an important element in your training, especially for those 45 or older.

The Perfect Sport for Not-So-Perfect Bodies

Autism, Muscular Dystrophy, and Juvenile Arthritis are just a few of the physical limitations that some of the students in my own school are living and training with. So how are they doing? The head instructor of my school was once told that he would never walk properly again, much less be athletic. As a third-degree black belt, he has won many national championships and is known for his exceptionally high kicking ability.

Another black belt instructor at my school was diagnosed with Muscular Dystrophy as a baby, and his parents were told he would be nothing more than a cripple for the rest of his life. Though he can't kick as high as he would probably like to, no one in class even knows that he has a physical limitation. These martial artists are exceptional examples of learning to overcome physical limitations through martial arts training.

Once again, you learn to work with what you have. If we have to hold the board a little lower for you to kick, then we will do so without penalizing you. In Tae Kwon Do, just because you can't soar through the air like a Power Ranger doesn't mean that you'll never get your black belt. Of course, you have to be realistic. Those with physical limitations will often have to train twice as long before being ready to even take their black belt test. But I guarantee you your instructor will not give up on you as long as you yourself remain dedicated. Time is not of the essence in your Tae Kwon Do training. Patience and dedication are.

The Least You Need to Know

➤ Psychologists and therapists have recommended Tae Kwon Do and other martial arts for children with behavioral problems or learning disabilities.

➤ A woman who trains in Tae Kwon Do is less likely to be victimized.

➤ Older students can and do hit hard!

➤ Students with physical limitations can still become a black belt.

Part 2
Kick-Start Your Training

Before you start making the actual moves, you need to understand some of the basic principles of the martial arts in general and in Tae Kwon Do in particular. The advantages and even the disadvantages of training can be recognized if you'll take a little time to investigate the many aspects of the arts.

Finding the Right School

You've decided to take the step. You want to sign up for Tae Kwon Do for yourself or maybe for your child. How in the world do you go about finding the right school? Well, when choosing a school, you must first understand clearly what you or your child expect to gain from learning Tae Kwon Do. You may want your child to learn self-confidence and respect while having fun at the same time. You may want to get shape while learning how to put some serious hurt on someone (purely in self-defense, of course). Then again, maybe you need the confidence and your kid needs to learn how to deal with the red-haired, freckle-faced bully who keeps smearing his face in the dirt at recess. Whatever your goals, the process for choosing a school is pretty much the same.

More than Just Fending Off Freckle-Face

You should realize there are many different types of schools and variations on instructors (even within the world of Tae Kwon Do). Even if your child does need to learn how to fend off freckle-face, you still may not want your child involved in a hard-core, full-contact, *Death-Blows-R-Us* school. These schools tend to be pretty rough and seem geared more toward adults with criminal records. Remember that you or your child has the right to learn effective self-defense skills from instructors who are as competent at their teaching and communication skills as they are at their Tae Kwon Do skills.

If you're looking for a little light recreation and fun, then a brief introduction to a self-defense program may suffice. If it's serious self-defense or personal development you are looking for, then you'll have to spend more than just a few lessons—a full-time, professionally run program will be more suitable.

With the unfortunate decline in the quality of education in America, many parents have come to view the martial arts as a necessary part of their child's personal and educational development. In any case, a good professional instructor can really help supplement your child's education and provide a much-needed form of exercise and personal development.

> **Watch Out, Grasshopper**
>
> You must show respect to the instructor at all times in class. For example, you should turn away from the instructor before making adjustments to your uniform or belt. Bow to the instructor when he addresses you personally. Never walk in front of an instructor, between her and the students.

Let Your Fingers Do the Walking

Start by asking around among your friends and family. The majority of students in many martial arts schools come from referrals from satisfied students and parents. If you don't know anyone currently involved, check out the Yellow Pages. The are probably a number of Tae Kwon Do schools, or Do Jangs, in your town or city. But don't judge a school by the size of their ad. Visit and watch the instructor work with other students and children.

As we have already said, every school is different because every instructor is different. And don't get confused by claims of multiple black-belt degrees, big tournament wins, or martial art styles. The only style that matters is the teaching style of the instructor and how you or your child will respond to him or her.

Looking at the phone-book ads it's almost impossible not to find a Tae Kwon Do champion. It sometimes seems every instructor in town claims to be a champion of some sort. However, like rank, tournament titles mean little to your level of satisfaction with your instructor. Just because someone has won an event doesn't mean he or she can teach you or your child. In fact, the hard-core competitor or coach often has a difficult time toning the training down for the novice or for kids. For instance, Jimmy Johnson is a great, Super-Bowl–winning, football coach, but would he be as good coaching seven-year-olds?

Wise Sa Bum Tells Us

If you're having doubts, call the Better Business Bureau to ask if there have been any complaints against the school you are thinking about. Teachers in a YMCA or city recreation center have been checked out by that organization and have to answer to their standards of conduct for employees.

What Does a Good Instructor Look Like?

The fact of the matter is, there are good and not-so-good practitioners in every profession, so what are some of the things you should look for in a good Tae Kwon Do instructor?

Believe it or not, all good instructors have a little "Sergeant Carter" in them. In Karate, if your instructor yells at you, it means he cares. The reason is, if an instructor sees someone with potential, he will correct and guide that individual because he sees that he has what it takes to make black belt. A good instructor will yell at you if he has to. And he'll stay on you to make even the tiniest little corrections. A sign of a good teacher is someone who won't turn the other way and let you get by with less than your best.

Children especially need to know the difference between right and wrong—not just in the Do Jang, but also in life. It is far easier to look the other way and not to take the time to correct a student. A good instructor will take the time to make you shape up.

Nag, Nag, Nag

I can remember a couple of hard lessons I've had to learn myself as I was climbing up the ranks. At times, my own instructor used to do things to make me think that he was picking on me. One time, there was a particular move that I just couldn't get. Over and over I would try while he stood behind me and told me that I was still doing it wrong. I got so frustrated that I started to cry and wanted to quit. Well I didn't quit, and I eventually got the move down, and I appreciate him sticking with me more than he'll ever know. He kept pushing me because he knew I had the potential to achieve something that I couldn't see. My instructor was teaching me to never quit no matter how tough things can get. It takes much more effort for a teacher to coach and guide a student than to turn his head and look the other way when she makes a mistake.

Get Out the Vacuum

Probably my greatest lesson was one of humility. Every day my instructor used to make me run the sweeper after class. It got to the point that I didn't even wait for him to ask, I just went to the back and pulled out the vacuum cleaner. Even today, I have no problem running the sweeper if he asks me to. Learning how to remain humble has probably furthered my professional life more than any other aspect I can think of. It keeps me grounded and it reminds me of what truth really is.

There are other qualities to look for in a good teacher. A good teacher will be repetitive. Bet you didn't realize that. You see, you might think it is monotonous, doing the same things over and over again. But the good instructor knows that repetition is the surest way to perfection. You have to realize that sometimes even a lifetime is not enough time to truly *master* martial arts. Besides, if you ever have to defend yourself, it will be those instantaneous reflexes that may save your life. And that's something that can only be achieved by doing one simple block a thousand times over.

By the same token, if class at times seems so challenging that you feel like you're going to pass out, be sure to thank your instructor because he's teaching you a great lesson about yourself. He's teaching you self-confidence and self-respect. The point is, you probably won't pass out, even though you are being pushed beyond what you think your limitations are. It's after those really tough classes that you feel good about yourself and start to respect yourself for making it through. In a nutshell, Tae Kwon Do cannot make a difference in your life if you don't have an instructor who's considered *driving*.

Looking Down from 10,000 Feet

Realize that as you train, your instructor is looking at the *big picture*. He knows that he has, on the average, barely four years to whip you in shape for the test that will change your life, the black belt test. Your endurance, technique, and skills have to be at a certain level, and this is largely the responsibility of the teacher.

If he cares, your instructor will do all of the things we just talked about; if he doesn't care, believe me, it's easy just to take your money and look the other way. The day you get your black belt, I guarantee you'll look at your instructor and smile—maybe even cry—and I just bet he'll smile back. If at no other point in your training you realize it, you will definitely realize at that moment that your instructor was truly working on your behalf over the years. That's why finding the right instructor is so important.

So What's a Prospective Student to Do?

The bottom line is to trust your instincts. Talk to the instructor and look around. A good school will have a family atmosphere, lots of smiles, and be well kept. The students will be impressive and enthusiastic. The mirrors are polished, the floor is clean, and the dressing rooms in good order. On the wall you might see photographs of recent school events and outings, and there should be an area for parents or family to sit and watch the classes. You should feel comfortable, not intimidated, with the personnel and the facility. If you walk in and the place is smelly and dirty, all the photos are of the instructor smashing bricks (or people) and the wall is covered with enough weapons to mount a small coup, you may want to look elsewhere.

However, if the school is clean with a bright, pleasant atmosphere, that's a step in the right direction. Still, the bottom line is the instructor/student relationship. You must find someone you can trust, respect, and feel comfortable with. It's one thing to respect an instructor because of the excellent and patient manner in which he or she works with your child. It's entirely different when your respect is based upon intimidation if you step out of line. When it comes to the safety and education of you or your child, an extra 10-minute drive can make a world of difference in the outcome.

Watch and Learn

Most instructors won't mind if you want to watch, especially if you are checking out schools. They know that once you see the positive lessons they are teaching your child, you'll be even more supportive of the training. You might even want to join in! But keep in mind that some children do not perform as well when Mom or Dad is standing in the back staring at them. Sometimes our own parents can make us nervous. If you find this to be the case, it's better that you leave them and pick them up after class.

Martial arts, taught by a good instructor, have a series of *victories* for each child ranging from a new belt or stripe on their belt to other forms of recognition for the child. Mom and/or Dad should definitely be present at these times. That recognition is greatly enhanced when the parent is there to share in the pride. Even if you never take a step out on the mat yourself, Tae Kwon Do can be a great experience to share with your children.

> **Martial Arts Minute**
> It is a Korean martial arts custom to shake with two hands when greeting someone. Likewise both hands should be extended when giving or receiving something from a fellow practitioner.

How Much Should Lessons Cost?

While the actual investment per month will vary widely from market to market, this question has to be approached from a slightly different perspective than money alone. What is your piece of mind worth? You can't put a price on your self-confidence as a woman walking to her car at night. What is it worth to a parent to know that his or her child is developing the self-pride and inner confidence to avoid negative peer pressures? What is it worth to any of us in today's violent world to empower ourselves or our children with the skills to handle a confrontation?

It's worth a lot more than it costs to gain the knowledge. With the huge variance in the instructors, facility, and atmosphere of one school to the next, you should never shop for the martial arts based upon price. Schools tend to charge what they think they are worth. If a school is charging less than everyone else in town, there's probably a reason. If a school is charging more than anyone else, they probably feel it is worth the price. Interestingly, the more expensive schools often have more students than the bargain basement ones. If the school charges less than $30 or more than $90 a month, ask why. I am not saying these are bad schools or teachers at all, just that they are out of the normal price ranges for classes.

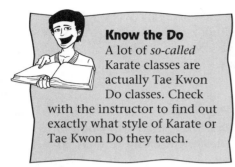

Know the Do
A lot of *so-called* Karate classes are actually Tae Kwon Do classes. Check with the instructor to find out exactly what style of Karate or Tae Kwon Do they teach.

While all good schools will allow you to pay a monthly fee for classes, some will also offer you a chance to pay for classes in advance, usually at a discount. Just be careful. There is a big difference between being offered the option to pay for, say a year in advance for a discount, and being told that advance payments are the only option. If a school insists that you must pay for more than 30 days in advance, do not enroll. This is a school, usually, that has a very high drop-out rate and they know you may not stick around for long, so they try get as much money as possible from you before you leave.

Most schools have a standard payment plan and then a small discount of 15 to 20 percent if you want to pay the full amount in advance. This is a reasonable option that is simply that, an option. If you decide to pay in advance, make sure you have a written agreement that's signed by the instructor as to what is being paid for and what would constitute cause for a refund. This is an example where signing a contract may be in your best interest. For instance, if you are in an automobile wreck or are transferred, is that cause for a refund? Your attorney would have the answer based upon the state you live in so be sure to investigate that and protect your investment before making advance payments.

How Long Are the Classes?

Watch Out, Grasshopper
Arriving late to class is frowned upon. You must stand at the edge of the mat or at the door to be acknowledged and *bowed in* by the instructor.

Classes are not necessarily more valuable if they are longer. Class length should depend on the age of the class. For most classes targeting four- to six-year-olds, the class should run 30 to 45 minutes. For older kids and adults, 45 minutes to an hour is pretty standard. Schools that have two-hour beginner classes tend to burn out their students very quickly. In today's world, it's just very difficult for busy people to devote more than an hour or so to an activity. And studies on attention spans have shown that 30 to 60 minutes are about the max for most people (depending on their age).

Will It Hurt?

How risky is martial arts training? According to insurance ratings based on the number of injury claims, you have a better chance getting hurt playing golf than practicing martial arts. That doesn't mean you're not going to get sore or occasionally bruised; it just means that serious injuries are not very common in the martial arts in most schools.

Most good schools with certified instructors are very safe and go to extreme lengths to insure the safety of their classes. Other schools are rougher and can have a military-like atmosphere where only the strong survive. These schools can be recognized by an almost exclusively adult male student body, which often look like attendees to a tattoo convention. Any school you attend should utilize the foam-padded safety equipment when sparring.

Should You Be a Sport?

Many instructors feel Tae Kwon Do should really be called a sport rather than a martial art because of the emphasis on competition (especially prevalent since Tae Kwon Do's inclusion in the Olympics). If you aren't particularly interested in the sporting aspects, talk to your potential teacher about it. You might have to find a school or instructor who plays down that area. There are schools that put a much higher emphasis on fighting, for instance. Fighting should not be the most important aspect in a student's training. Be sure to ask the instructor questions like this.

Certification?

Contrary to the media's image of a tough, no-smiles martial arts instructor, today's instructors are generally a little kinder and gentler (at least at first). They will be certified by their parent organization and will probably even have some further training in communication and motivational skills. Just a note here: While certification is valuable, there is no single governing body for the martial arts. Most modern federations and associations, however, have set up standards for instructors.

This emphasis on personal responsibility and successful attitudes was introduced into the martial arts classroom in the mid-1980s and has come as a pleasant surprise to many students who feared that martial arts would be a *survival of the fittest* experience. Of course, those schools still exist; you just have to do a little research to find the right teacher for you. Today students of all ages and athletic ability should be able to train in the martial arts.

Know the Do
You already know that *Sa Bum* means teacher. *Kwan Jang Nim* means the head or founder of a style.

It's Work After All

In spite of all I've just said about fun and family atmosphere in the Do Jang, Tae Kwon Do is, and should be, hard work. It's not recess. It is learning how to punch, kick, and perhaps, in the worst-case scenario, protect yourself or your loved ones in a real confrontation. Martial arts are all about self-confidence and self-improvement, but that's only achieved through lots of sweat, effort, and sore muscles.

There is nothing quite like the satisfaction of a strenuous workout where you not only have stretched and strengthened your muscles but have also stretched your mind and strengthened your self-discipline. Ultimately you will get to that point if you stick with it.

The good teacher will make it easy enough at first and will make sure you get encouragement along the way.

The Least You Need to Know

➤ The teaching style of the instructor is much more important than any fancy certificates or trophies he or she might have.

➤ Don't shop a potential school by price but by what it can provide for you.

➤ Plan on spending on hour in class two or three times a week.

➤ It's going to be fun, but it's also going to be hard work.

Chapter 6

The Big Welcome Mat

In This Chapter

➤ Knowing what to expect

➤ Discovering what your school will be like

➤ Getting off on the right foot with your instructor

➤ Treating your fellow students with respect

Okay, you're finally here. You know how to find an instructor and a school you will feel comfortable with and you're ready to learn about the classroom for the first time. Most new students have no idea what to expect and are naturally a little nervous. (Should I say scared?) But because you've read this book you know what to look out for.

For serious students of Tae Kwon Do, the school becomes like a second home, an oasis of calm in an otherwise hectic life. When you enter through those doors, you leave your everyday concerns outside. All are treated equally here. There is no status except the one you earn by training diligently and climbing the ranks. In the outside world you may be a grandmother or a fraternity brother, a trash collector or a Supreme Court justice, but within the four walls of the school, you're simply a student like everyone else, training side by side with those of both higher and lower rank.

Inside the Do Jang

Your first class in the Do Jang may be an unforgettable experience, but your first glance at this room may not be so impressive. Traditionally speaking, the Do Jang isn't much more than a floor, a ceiling, and four walls. Of course more modern schools have become widespread in the Western world. Many have vinyl mats, full-length mirrors, showers, and separate men's and women's dressing rooms. But whether your Do Jang rivals the finest health facilities or is a simple storefront or even the corner YMCA, you'll be amazed to find how much significance this simple space will come to hold in your life.

Another tradition of the Do Jang is that the place is to be kept immaculate. It is a sacred space, much like a church. Of course what makes it so special is the hard work and the reverence of those who train there, day after day and year after year. Even the least experienced students usually sense this, and never have to be reminded to help keep their Do Jang spotless. It is not uncommon to see white belts polishing the mirrors or sweeping the mat. In fact, in the old country it was a requirement for promotion.

Wise Sa Bum Tells Us

If you see something that needs to be cleaned in the Do Jang or even just a simple chore like moving the chairs so the next group of spectators can sit for class, you should jump to do the task. Your teachers will certainly notice your behavior and will take note that you have the proper martial spirit of humility and service.

The Condiments

There are many different types of schools, both in a physical sense and in a metaphysical sense. Some are run like a military academy. Some have a cheery, upbeat attitude of a health resort. The ideal Do Jang is actually a bit of both. It should be strict; after all, you are learning a *martial* art. But it should also be a place where you want to come, a place where you can learn in an environment that is conducive to learning.

One of the ways to improve the learning experience is to have things in the Do Jang that will aid in your lessons. As I have already mentioned, many schools have mirrors on the walls. This is a great way to check out your form (not your body, but your execution of technique). Your Do Jang may have hanging, heavy bags on which you can practice your kicks and punches. Since you are not allowed to kick the other white belts in the stomach, this bag serves as a good substitute. Some bags are filled with sawdust and are hard as a rock. Some of the more modern bags have water-filled cores that have the consistency and give of an actual human body.

Heavy bag in the Do Jang.

The traditional floor is wood, but many modern Do Jangs have a soft, vinyl mat stretched over the workout area or are even carpeted. This aids in softening the falls (Tae Kwon Do is not a throwing art so you shouldn't be hitting the mat often, if at all). There may be a spectator area and an office for the instructor. Stay out of both of these areas unless you have a reason to be there.

Dressing rooms are another modern addition to the traditional Do Jang. Needless to say, keep them clean (no one wants to pick up or even have to look at your dirty underwear). Bring your own towels and help keep the floors dry.

The Unwritten Rules

You might think, "If they want me to obey these rules they should write them down!" And, indeed, in some schools there are signs and posters on the walls listing the "Rules of the Do Jang." But in many schools the traditions are passed on from senior to junior students. After a while you just know what to do, and what not to.

For one thing, before you enter the Do Jang, take off your shoes and place them in a designated spot just outside the Do Jang floor. Everyone from the lowliest beginner to the most highly respected black belt shows his or her respect for the place of study. Of course, it's also a great way to keep the floors clean. And speaking of which, be sure to wash your feet before you come to class. There is nothing more noticeable than black, dirty feet when everyone is working out bare-footed.

Follow the instructor closely in the Do Jang.

Inside the Do Jang, you'll notice that one wall is covered with flags: a Korean flag to the right, an American flag on the left, and in some cases a federation flag between the two. This is considered the front of the room. When students line up to train, they always face the flags.

Know the Do
Sheejak is the Korean word for begin. You'll be beginning a lot of stuff (kicks, forms, etc.) during your training.

By the way, it's important to bow to the Do Jang and/or flags any time you enter or exit the Do Jang. This is done in different ways, depending on what the school specifies. Some schools require a simple bow while others require that you place your right hand over your heart while bowing.

And speaking of bowing at the entrance, if for some reason you arrive late, take off your shoes, then stand at the door and wait for the instructor to acknowledge you. (Calling out his name or entering without permission is considered the height of bad form.) When he notices you, ask, "Permission to join class, sir." If permission is granted (and it probably will be unless you make a habit of this sort of thing), you must line up at the back of the class, regardless of your rank.

That being said, don't take the opposite approach and show up half an hour early. Though your dedication is appreciated, your instructor has a life too, and he's not sitting around all day waiting for you to make an appearance. If you need to come to class early for some reason, always call ahead to check.

Parents, make sure your kids never arrive more than 15 minutes prior to class (unless the instructor specifically requests it). Forcing the instructors to baby-sit is not only improper but rude.

Martial Arts Minute
In the early days of martial arts in this country (the 1950s and '60s), no one knew the rules of etiquette and respect for black belts. It was not uncommon for "thugs" to come in off the street and challenge the instructor in a Do Jang. More often than not that was a big mistake. There are stories of bloody noses and even broken bones being the result of such challenges.

Master and Student

Building a good relationship with your instructor is probably the single most important factor in how much enjoyment and success you find in your training. Like every other aspect of Tae Kwon Do, this relationship is bound by years of tradition. Before you ever step into the classroom, it's helpful to understand that as relationships go, this should be a pretty formal one. This is a hard concept to grasp for many Westerners. After all, we live in a free-and-easy society where waiters introduce themselves to customers and even bosses and employees operate on a first-name basis.

Over years of training you will certainly come to think of your instructor as "Mr. Smith" or "Ms. Jones," or whatever his or her name may be, and you wouldn't even think of saying, "Hey Bob." But at first you may have to make sure you remember this unwritten rule.

Don't Put Your Foot in Your Mouth

I remember the first day that I signed up for lessons. I asked my instructor what his name was and he said, "Mr. Bruno." "Yeah, but what does everybody call you?" I asked. "Everybody calls me Mr. Bruno." Of course I didn't realize at the time what that unwritten rule was. In fact all black belts, not just the senior instructor, are referred to as "Mr.," "Miss," or "Mrs." The really high-ranking black belts, those holding the title of Master or Grand-master, may even wish you to address them using those titles. It may seem a little weird, especially if your instructor is younger than you are, but that's just the way it works.

Incidentally, when it's a child who holds a black belt, the rules may be slightly different. Some schools allow you to refer to the child as "Mr." or "Miss," followed by their first name, for example, "Mr. Pete" or "Miss Kathy." Other Do Jangs require all black belts be addressed as "Mr. Jones." Check on the rules of your school before speaking to even a young black belt. Since children generally aren't permitted to teach, you probably won't run into this situation your first night out.

When the instructor enters the Do Jang, the highest-ranked student present will call the class to attention. After everyone rises, the highest-ranked student will give the command *Sa Bum Nim Kay Kyung Ret* (Korean for "bow to the master"). Some schools also follow the bow with a brotherhood greeting like "Tae Kwon!"

Watch Out, Grasshopper
Under no circumstances should you call your instructor by his first name or, heaven forbid, anything else like "Man" or "Mr. Martial Arts Dude." You might be sweeping the Do Jang floors for the next year!

Know the Do
When you add the suffix "nim" to a word, as in Sa Bum Nim, it's kind of like saying "san" in Japanese to indicate a high level of respect or admiration. (Remember "Daniel-san" in *The Karate Kid*?)

In some cases, your instructor may be on the Do Jang mat when you arrive; for example, if he's just finished giving a private lesson. In this situation, it is proper to greet him right away, before you do anything else. You don't have to say anything, just wait until his eyes meet yours and bow, bending forward at the waist.

If you've been training with an instructor for a while, you may be tempted to strike up a conversation with him. In most cases, this isn't recommended since it tends to undermine the traditional Asian teacher/student relationship. Wait for him to address you first.

Getting personal with your instructor is considered a major faux pas in any martial art. Questions like "Are you married?" or "How's business?" are considered too personal. Joking or sarcastic comments like "You seem to be in a better mood today," or "Smile, will ya?" are considered to be poor etiquette. However, questions like "Are you feeling better?" (if he's been laid up with a cold) or, "Is there anything I can do to help?" are perfectly okay, since they show basic human concern.

If you're with me so far, you're probably wondering, "Is all this formality really necessary? Can't you just learn the moves without crossing all the t's and dotting all the i's?" No, you really can't. It adds to the whole Do Jang experience. It introduces the elements of discipline and respect that we've already talked about being so important to your training. Imagine if all kids started calling their elders "sir" and "ma'am." It might change the whole educational system of this country.

As I've said before, there's more to studying Tae Kwon Do than learning a bunch of kicks and blocks. To really practice this ancient martial art, you've got to train your mind and spirit as well, which means embracing a way of thinking and behaving that may seem foreign to you at first. It's a leap of faith, but you've got to take that leap. You will soon be glad you did.

When to Ask, When to Shut Up

It is also an Asian custom that you do not question authority. In our culture, of course, it is a little different. Remember that when you do Tae Kwon Do you are doing an *Asian* thing; therefore, Asian customs are in order.

For example, during class there will be times when you may not understand something, like why a certain move has to be done in a particular way. Nine times out of 10 your instructor will explain his reasons, or they'll become clear when you actually apply the technique. If not, save your questions for after class, when you can speak with the instructor privately. It's considered disrespectful to question the teacher's instructions in class. Under most circumstances, classroom commands should be answered with a spirited "Yes, sir," or "Yes, ma'am."

The instructor is there to help you perfect your techniques.

Martial Arts Minute
In traditional Korean arts, most instructors will not pal around with their students. Not because they don't want to, but because they know that keeping a certain distance between student and teacher is a must for keeping the mutual respect.

Another way students show respect is by asking for permission before leaving class. If you're getting sick or absolutely must go to the bathroom, always ask before exiting the Do Jang floor. In fact, as you progress, you should always ask for your instructor's permission before showing or teaching any junior belt anything.

If you have a less immediate request (you'd like to stay and practice after class has been dismissed, or you want permission to train in the Do Jang outside of normal class hours), save your question for after class and approach the instructor in his office. In these cases, always knock first, and don't enter until you're asked to come in. Stand at attention until you're given permission to sit, then make your request. If permission is granted, bow and exit. If permission is not granted, don't ask why, and don't argue back. Just bow and exit.

Tae Kwon Dos

Here is a list of things you should do:

➤ Be on time. It shows that you take your training seriously.

➤ Make an effort to learn the Korean terms. It's part of your Tae Kwon Do training.

➤ Take off your shoes before entering the Do Jang—or the instructor's office.

➤ Have clean feet! Everyone must take his shoes off to train.

Tae Kwon Don'ts

Here is a list of things you should not do:

➤ Don't ask to go to the bathroom unless absolutely necessary.

➤ Don't ask to rest unless you're feeling sick.

➤ Don't chew gum in class.

➤ Don't ask to get a drink of water, unless you've got some serious hiccups.

➤ Don't ask to be dismissed early unless you've cleared it with your instructor beforehand.

Becoming a Dedicated Student

How often you're expected to train varies from one school to another. Some schools are very strict about scheduling and ask you to commit to exactly which days you'll attend class.

Others are more flexible. Most instructors recommend you come at least twice a week, not much considering that most classes are only an hour long. In fact, it's common for schools to set a quota for class attendance. If you don't meet this quota (say, 10 classes a month), you may be held back from testing for your next belt rank.

As a general rule, I'd say that unless you're preparing for a competition, training three days a week is plenty. Tae Kwon Do teaches your body to move in new and unfamiliar ways, and even if you're in very good shape, your muscles will need time off between classes to repair themselves. I've seen compulsive personalities come in to train every day, day after day. I've never seen one of them make it to black belt.

If you're going out of town for a week or more, be sure to let your instructor know. Believe it or not, he does notice when you're not there and may worry about you. If he hasn't seen you in class for a while, don't be surprised if your instructor calls to ask where you've been.

The easiest way to get off on the right foot with your instructor is to be on time for class. Sounds pretty obvious, but you'd be amazed by how often new students blow it. Late-comers disrupt the flow of the class and distract their fellow students. (Remember the rules about coming in late.)

Wise Sa Bum Tells Us

Try to arrive five or 10 minutes before class starts. This gives you time to take off your shoes, get yourself into the right mental state, and give yourself a few minutes to stretch.

Gift Giving Etiquette

You won't be held back from promotions if you don't give your teacher gifts. And trust me, he's not expecting anything, but gift giving has been a long-standing Oriental custom of showing one's appreciation. Nothing too expensive or personal, just a simple token of your appreciation, such as a book your instructor is likely to enjoy—like this one. It's not expected of you, but giving a small gift during the holidays or any time the instructor has given you special help or encouragement just shows your respect.

If you're a product of American public schools like I am, this may feel like brown-nosing, but, take my word for it, within the martial arts tradition it's quite common, and your instructor won't think you're kissing up to him.

As an instructor, I have been deeply moved by this kind of expression. Children are the greatest teachers when it comes to gift giving. I've been inspired by the simplicity and sincerity of kids who, unbeknownst to their parents, have brought me favorite rocks, pennies, marbles, or just about anything else they thought was pretty neat. Probably the most touching gift I've ever received was a stuffed dog. It came from a little girl who lived in my neighborhood and had heard that my dog had died.

The Pecking Order

The rules for dealing with your fellow classmates aren't quite as strict as the master/student relationship, but some rules do exist here as well. This is especially true when you're dealing with students of a higher rank.

Many new students are surprised to find themselves training alongside those who've been practicing Tae Kwon Do for many years, instead of in a true beginners' class. There's a reason for this. Seeing higher-ranked students in action helps beginners understand the belt system and gain an appreciation of rank. It also gives them something to aspire to.

Watch Out, Grasshopper
Although technically you don't have to bow to anyone but black belts, it's probably a good idea to show your respect with a bow to any student above you. And if you *don't* bow to the black belts, you could get into real trouble.

Of course, this can be intimidating at first; but a student who's trained long and hard enough to attain a brown or black belt understands the spirit of Tae Kwon Do and knows better than to rub your nose in your mistakes. In fact, one of the duties of an upper belt is to help out the lower-ranked students. This is usually done out of genuine love and concern for those coming up the ranks. Bottom line: These folks can be great sources of inspiration and encouragement. Don't pass up these valuable relationships. And remember, everyone started out as a white belt.

All students are expected to greet each other before class. The greeting is initiated by the lower-ranked student. To do this, wait until the other person's eyes meet yours, then bow. (If you're both wearing the same color belt, either one of you can make the first move.) This shows mutual respect.

The same applies for saying good-bye at the end of class. A simple bow will do. Some schools follow it up with a brotherhood greeting.

Wise Sa Bum Tells Us
If a black belt student enters the Do Jang after class has started, all students are expected to turn and bow. And don't forget that all black belts, not just the senior instructor, should be addressed with a "sir" or "ma'am."

At the beginning of every class the students line up according to rank. White belts are on the left with the upper-most ranks at the right. In a group of all the same belt color (orange belt, for example) the children line up to the left of the adults.

If this all seems hard, just remember this basic philosophy: treat each man as your brother and each woman as your sister. Every person in the Do Jang is to be treated equally and respectfully. If you keep this in mind, you can't go wrong.

Taking the Do Jang Rules Out on the Street

What many new students don't realize is that all these rules apply outside the Do Jang as well. Let's say you run into your instructor at the mall. Believe it or not, you should come to attention and bow just as you normally would at the school. The reality is that your instructor does venture outside of the school. He has to shop, eat, and fill his gas tank just like everybody else. Should you run into him in public, always show proper respect.

A young student of mine who happens to live down the road from me demonstrated one great example of this. While I was out walking my dog, this young boy ran to retrieve his ball. Once he made eye contact with me, he immediately let the ball go, came to attention, and bowed.

The same goes for your classmates. Whether you meet at the bus stop or the corner deli, stop and bow. It may feel odd at first, but remember that you're part of a brotherhood. Be proud of it!

Speaking of your fellow students, I'd be remiss if I didn't warn you about a mistake that can have a disastrous effect on your and your classmates' training. Dating a fellow student. The Do Jang is not a singles' bar! Getting romantically involved with a fellow student is definitely frowned upon. It becomes very awkward if and when the relationship doesn't work out. It sometimes forces one or both of the students to quit.

Some schools are very strict about this. I know of more than one situation where both students were asked to leave because they became romantically involved. Whether or not the relationship works out, I've seen it create serious tension in the classroom. Dating a classmate is a lot like dating a co-worker; it just isn't worth the risk.

I Fought the Law, and the Law Won

Along these same lines, how you conduct yourself in public definitely affects your standing in the martial arts community. You're expected to abide by not only the rules and traditions of Tae Kwon Do but society's rules as well. Being a law-abiding citizen is par for the course. Disorderly conduct in life can result in being kicked out of your school.

These standards apply to children as well. Kids who study Tae Kwon Do are taught to respect authority not just in the Do Jang, but at home and at school. If the instructor learns that one of his students has been a holy terror at home or has mouthed off to his teachers at school, you can bet that child will be put on notice. Parents are often pleasantly surprised to learn that the martial arts instructor can be a powerful ally in teaching a child respect and discipline. Even kids who don't respond to parental discipline usually buckle down rather than face the reproach of the Tae Kwon Do master.

Finally, you'll want to be particularly careful not to brag about your training, since this kind of idle boasting has led to more than a few street fights and bar brawls. Once you learn the ins and outs of fighting, you began to realize that giving demonstrations of your ability outside of the classroom only invites the insecure and uninformed to try and challenge you. It's not worth it. Your martial arts training is a sacred thing. When it comes to the outside world, only use it if you have to, and leave the bragging to others.

The Least You Need to Know

➤ Always remove your shoes before entering the Do Jang.

➤ Avoid getting personal with your instructor.

➤ Greet your instructor and fellow students with a bow, whether you meet in class or on the street.

➤ If you want to, it's okay to give your instructor gifts.

➤ Don't take the risk of dating fellow students. Your love life is best left outside the Do Jang.

➤ Never brag about your training.

Chapter 7

Fright Night: Your First Class

In This Chapter

➤ Starting out in private lessons and graduating to the big class

➤ Knowing what will be expected of you

➤ Finding out how hard it will be

➤ Learning how to relax and have fun

Remember your first day at kindergarten? If that's too far back, how about your first day in high school, or college, or how about your wedding day? Certain days stick out in your mind as anxiety producing—no, a better word would be *frightening*.

Certainly your first night in the Do Jang would qualify as a scary experience. Even if the instructor has assured you that you won't be singled out. Even if you have some friends taking the class with you. It's still kinda nerve-wracking to have to put on that white uniform and stand in a row, at attention, like a little kid.

But don't worry. We're going to walk you through what to expect and how to act. You'll handle it like a veteran black belt...well, as least a green belt.

Doing It in Private?

Many schools will let you take a "try before you buy" private lesson or two before you make an obligation to sign up for regular classes. In the more traditional Do Jangs (with rigidly run class curriculums), private lessons are a must since you'll find it difficult to just come in and join a regular class.

Usually the senior instructor will teach your private lessons; however, he may designate another black belt or advanced student to help out. Don't worry, he's not going to stick you with someone who doesn't have the patience, or can't handle the situation. In fact, private lessons are often so fun that you may ask, "Why can't I be in private lessons for the rest of my martial arts career?" Because learning to respect those above and below you is all part of the martial arts experience, and you just can't learn to respect others, or ultimately respect yourself, if you don't participate in a regular class.

Yes, you'll be insecure and even humbled when you must first join "the group," but this is the foundation for the coming lessons in building your own confidence and self-esteem. So let's get ready.

What's It Like?

The average adult class is around an hour long and falls into several *segments*. They are as follows:

1. You'll start with the opening ceremonies like saluting flags, bowing to instructor, meditation, etc.

2. Then you'll do warm-up exercises such as neck exercises, knee exercises, and leg stretching. During this first class segment you pretty much warm up each and every large muscle group. Then there should be some form of cardio-exercise like jumping jacks, laps, or simple punching and kicking drills (don't worry, they'll be easy with you in your first class).

> **Martial Arts Minute**
> In the old days, kids and adults worked out together. Today however, most schools have specific classes just for children. How are they different? Many are only 30 to 45 minutes long and they include more fun and games. Still, this is martial arts, and discipline and respect is required at all times.

3. Then you'll move on to the learning segment of class. You will practice the basic techniques required for your next belt promotion, and you'll learn your kicks, punches, and forms (prearranged patterns of offensive and defensive moves).

4. Some classes have a period of special instruction. This can include things like self-defense practice, board-breaking, or special drills to work on a particular skill like balance or power.

5. Sparring practice is usually held toward the end of class (first-timers do not spar).

6. Often a period of endurance exercise is included, such as push-ups, sit-ups, or other exercises.

7. Finally it's back to the etiquette of the closing ceremony with bows and thank yous.

Okay, now that you kind of understand the sequence, let's go into a little more detail about each part of class, what to expect, and how to make it through without embarrassing yourself this first time out.

The Early Bird Catches the Worm

Well, you may not be catching any worms, but it still pays to get to class early. Not only to make yourself feel more comfortable with the surroundings and people but also to let the instructors know you are ready and waiting to go.

By the same token, don't show up too early—you may be interfering with your instructor's schedule. The simple solution is to ask when it is a good time for you to arrive for class. Unless otherwise specified, usually there's no need to show up early for private lessons. Adult students are normally expected no sooner than 30 minutes before class starts. Children will normally be asked to come to class no more than 15 minutes prior to starting time. (Remember, your instructor is not a baby-sitter!)

Outside of a tragedy, like you were just in an accident, tardiness is a big no-no. Sometimes a penalty is issued for those who are late for class. If the problem persists, you can expect a good old-fashioned yelling at by your teacher, and that can hurt worse than getting a beating!

Watch Out, Grasshopper
If you *do* show up late, don't try to sneak into class without being noticed—you'll really be doing push-ups then! Wait at the door for the instructor to bow you in (since you missed the initial bow-in ceremony).

Line Up

Most instructors will call out something like, "Line up," or "One line," to signify the start of class. You should run, not walk, to the very end of left side of the line since this is your first night. The only people on your left would be other first-nighters who are younger than you (specifically little kids). If you are a kid, then it's the end of the line for you.

In some situations where there isn't enough room for everyone to stand in a single line (a small room or a huge class), you might line up in two or even more lines. The same rules apply. Beginning students at the left and on the back row. More advanced students to the right and in front. Some schools allow all black belts to be in a line facing the students while other schools permit only the senior instructor at the front and the other junior black belts at the end of the student line.

Know the Do
Chunbi is the word for the ready position. *Charyo* is attention, and *kyungye* means to bow.

Remember to stand at the ready position and wait for further commands. If this seems kind of militaristic to you, it is. After all these are the military (martial) arts. If you used to be in the army, this won't seem strange. If you never got any closer to military service than watching old John Wayne movies on late-night TV, this is going to be an adjustment.

Students in ready position.

When to Bow and When to Rise

At the attention command, everyone brings their left foot up against their right and slaps their hands against their thighs with a loud snap. Remember to continue looking straight ahead and resist the temptation to look around to see what everyone else is doing.

At the command to bow, that's just what you do. But do it slowly and with your head bowed while you look at the floor in front of your feet. It is considered disrespectful to raise from the bow before the instructor does. You don't want to be standing up while he or she is still in the bow. Of course if you are bent over, you can't really tell if the instructor has raised up or not can you? The solution is just to bow really slow. After a while you'll get the hang of when to rise and when to stay bowed.

Wise Sa Bum Tells Us

Some styles of martial arts insist that the bow be done with the head down to show maximum respect. Others say that if you aren't looking at your opponent he might kick you in the face while you are looking at the ground. These schools bow respectfully but with the head slightly up. Actually, whichever way your school does it, you shouldn't really focus on the floor even if your eyes are lowered. Instead try to see everything around you using your peripheral vision. That's something you will develop as you train.

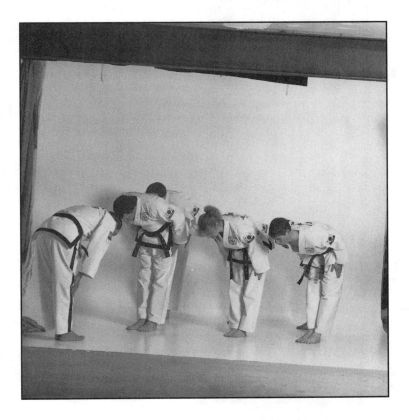

Students bowing at the start of class.

That's Quite a Spread You've Got There

After the bow the instructor will say something like, "Spread out!" meaning that you are about to start your warm-up period. Don't stand too close to the person next to you since you'll be doing everything from jumping jacks to swinging kicks. You might want to position yourself so you can see what the instructor is demonstrating. Looking at the instructor is permitted; however, try not to look at the other students. (If this is your first class the teachers will be a little more lenient about your looking around, but try to focus just on what you are supposed to be doing and not on what others are doing.)

Most Do Jangs will have mirrors on the walls. While that is good for checking out your techniques, it can be bad if you are looking in the glass when someone else gets too close with their kick or vice versa. Students have been known to kick one another in the butt while looking at themselves in the mirror. Sure, they are there for a reason, but use some common sense when you are in a crowded classroom.

Maintain the Position

If for some reason the instructor is momentarily called away during class (perhaps to talk to a visitor), you must hold your current position until given the next command. This is considered part of your training in learning discipline.

And let's say you are given the command to do 20 punches, and because you are particularly fast, you finish before everyone else. Stay in position. Don't relax and stand up straight waiting for all those other slow pokes. Remember the military, remember discipline!

I Don't Get It

Even if you follow along the best you can, there will come a point when you just don't get what they want you to do. Maybe it's a fancy kick or just a simple exercise. Don't be afraid to ask. Of course, don't just shout out, "Hey, I don't get it." Quietly raise your hand and wait for the instructor to call on you. When recognized you should politely bow and request clarification on the technique. However, the best advice for you if you just don't get it is to just do it anyway.

After it is explained, you should again bow and say something like, "Thank you, Sa Bum." Make sure you do understand what he wants you to do. Some students are afraid to ask too many questions (and of course, some do), but by and large the instructors want to show you in such a manner that you understand what is required. Some schools do have etiquette about going through the chain of command before asking a question, so be sure to check that out too.

Do Your Best

Some of the exercises you will see the other students doing will look absurdly hard. Push-ups on the knuckles? Stretch your legs out in a Chinese split? "Who do these people think they are? And they expect *me* to do that?" Well, not on your first night of course (although you might be amazed at the number of people who are able to do many of the martial arts exercises right off). Remember that the teachers and all your fellow students want you to have a good time, and above all they want to help you learn the art that they have learned to love. That means you should just relax, do your best, and try to have some fun. No one will get onto you for trying. Yes, it seems intimidating, but just remember that all the others in the room (even the Grandmaster himself) were once first-nighters.

First-nighters don't have to stretch out like these advanced students can.

Change of Pace

Although there is something to be said for consistency and predictability, the good instructor will change the pace of class every once in a while. Usually before a test or tournament, the class structure will change to gear toward what's necessary. For example, board-breaking may be practiced in class before a test. There may be more sparring and fighting drills in class, or more time spent on forms practice before a tournament to get students ready to compete.

The point is, expect to be challenged in class every time you set foot in the door and not just for your first night or two. Isn't that why you signed up in the first place? If you ever feel that your training has become boring or unchallenging, that's your fault. You need to make it more challenging by pushing yourself farther and higher every time you set foot in class.

Write It Down?

Some students find that they remember things better if they write them down, and that certainly is an option. But do it at home after class. Don't ask your instructor if he will write down everything he's taught you in that class. The way the martial arts have been taught for generations, in the Orient first and then in America, is by word of mouth. Besides, Asian instructors tend to get a little ticked if you can't seem to follow their verbal instructions without writing them down.

Safe at Last

Okay, you've been here for 45 minutes or an hour and it's almost the end. Usually sparring practice is reserved for the last class segment. Since you are a first-timer you won't have to get up there and fight. So possibly you may be able to just sit down safely on the sidelines and watch the other students do their stuff. But don't start to reflect on your first night experiences just yet. You can learn a lot by just watching the more advanced students sparring. You too will be up there soon enough, so watch how the students move. Watch how the instructor controls the match. Notice who seems to be getting in most of his or her techniques and how. Actually this is the most fun time of class for many students, not only sparring themselves but getting to watch the others spar. In many instances, the instructor may have you do some rudimentary sparring just to get you started.

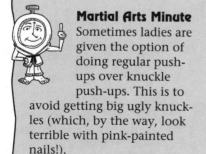

Martial Arts Minute
Sometimes ladies are given the option of doing regular push-ups over knuckle push-ups. This is to avoid getting big ugly knuckles (which, by the way, look terrible with pink-painted nails!).

The End

When class time is over the master will call the class to line up just as he did at the beginning. You should line up in the same manner as before. Some schools have a closing saying like, "Might for right," or "Tae Kwon." Just follow along and you'll learn it soon enough. The bowing commands are the same as in the beginning. In most Do Jangs you will do some more knuckle push-ups at the end (anywhere from 10 to 50). Why? Knuckle push-ups are a way of conditioning your knuckles. Should you ever have to make contact with your fist in a self-defense situation, you want to make sure you don't end up breaking your hand instead.

Knuckle push-ups.

Don't Forget Your Thank Yous

As soon as everyone bows out, it's a good idea to go around to those who helped you in class and say your thank yous. Don't forget the junior and senior instructors either. You'll never understand (at least not until you become an instructor yourself) the satisfaction that comes from knowing that you have helped a first-nighter feel comfortable and actually learn something.

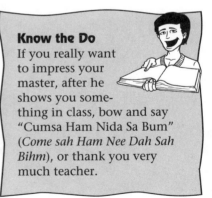

Know the Do

If you really want to impress your master, after he shows you something in class, bow and say "Cumsa Ham Nida Sa Bum" (*Come sah Ham Nee Dah Sah Bihm*), or thank you very much teacher.

The Least You Need to Know

➤ Be dressed properly and be early to your first class.

➤ Line up at the very end of the line and patiently wait for the bowing commands.

➤ If you don't understand something, raise your hand and ask.

➤ Just relax and try to do your best. Everyone is pulling for you to succeed.

Chapter 8

Looking the Part:
Your Uniform

In This Chapter

➤ Understanding why a clean uniform so important

➤ Determining the style you want to set

➤ Finding how many patches you can sew on

➤ Knowing when to say good-bye to a good friend

Every kid, and dare we say, every adult student, can't wait to try on their first "outfit." That simple white piece of clothing is the uniform of the martial artist. When you put it on you feel like the Karate Kid and the wise old Grandmaster all rolled into one.

In the Asian mindset, the way a man looks can reveal more about him than what meets the eye. Having a good appearance is a reflection of who he is and how he lives life. That's why the uniform of the martial artist is so important.

Looks Count

Sure, you can't judge a book by its cover, but sometimes you can judge a person's attitude by how he keeps himself. A soiled and sloppy appearance doesn't say much for how a man views himself and does say volumes about his pride and discipline.

If nothing else, as an honored representative of your school and federation, you should take pride in how you look in your uniform for the sake of your fellow students and instructors. Besides, just wearing a sharp-looking martial arts uniform gets you in a psychological frame of mind to do your best kicks and punches.

Classy As a Three-Piece Suit

> **Know the Do**
> In the early days of martial arts in this country, everyone, Tae Kwon Doists included, called the uniforms by the Japanese term *gi* (gee). As more and more Korean stylists have entered the scene, you hear the Korean word *dobak* (or *tobak*) in the Korean-style schools.

Tae Kwon Do uniforms are usually white, amplifying the traditional clothing of Korea. It is a three-piece affair: jacket, pants, and belt. They are available in light-, medium-, and heavy-weight fabrics. They can be polyester or cotton canvas. The heavy-weight uniforms are more durable but tend to be a bit more "challenging" than the light- or medium-weight ones. These heavy things can become possessed when you wash them. Like a pair of jeans, they are twice as stiff and twice as heavy when you get them wet. Taking my uniform out of the washer, you'd swear somebody was still in them. Honestly, I've lost my temper more while taking my uniform out of the washer than I have at any other aspect of my training. Yet day in and day out I will do what I have to to see that my uniform looks like a million bucks come next training session.

Men and women wear the same uniform.

Uniforms come in a variety of styles and colors (traditionally only black and white, however).

Pull Over or Wrap Around?

Originally the traditional uniform for martial artists was comprised of off-white, almost yellow, calf-length pants with a wrap-around jacket. There were little strings at each end of the jacket you could tie to keep the jacket together. Today the uniform has gotten whiter and longer (the pants now reach all the way to the ankles).

The South Korean Olympic schools of Tae Kwon Do have designed a new pull-over dobak that is a little harder to get on than the traditional wrap-around jacket, but it doesn't pull open in a vigorous workout or during self-defense practice in class. For this reason, many women prefer the pull-over style.

Watch Out, Grasshopper
Cross the left lapel over the right when putting on your uniform. Many students have been reprimanded for tying their top or belt the wrong way.

The pull-over dobak.

What Size?

Different brands of uniforms come in slightly different sizes, but generally speaking, a six- or seven-year-old is going to wear a size one or two uniform. Size three is for a bigger kid, maybe over 100 pounds. Size four is for a man or woman about 5'5" or 5'6". Size five is for those 5'10" or above. Uniforms come in sizes ranging all the way from size zero (a little-bitty kid) to size seven (a pro football player). Needless to say, you must check the size chart of the brand you are going to purchase. The cheaper uniforms come in a set, but in the more expensive versions you can mix and match different size tops and bottoms.

It is not uncommon for young students still growing to go through two or three different uniforms by the time they reach black belt. Moms are used to this, however, with kids often growing out of their shoes or pants before they have even been broken in.

Bells and Whistles

You'll notice that some uniforms are trimmed in colors. In some schools you are allowed green color lapels at a green belt, red lapels at red belt, and so on. Competition-style uniforms are permitted in some schools where you can mix colored pants with a white jacket, for example. Just like patches, there are certain rules about what color trim and pants you can wear, so be sure you know what is allowed in your Do Jang.

Sometimes women will secure the top of their uniform together by sewing on Velcro, so chances are, if you think you just heard a rip and thought that you've ripped a woman's top during practice, you have probably just loosened the Velcro. Incidentally, using safety pins to keep the top of your uniform together is not recommended since they can easily become loosened during rough training. Ouch!

Patches, Patches

Americans like bumper stickers on their cars and patches on their caps and windbreakers. Why should Tae Kwon Do uniforms be any different? Well, it is different in that you'd better follow the rules set up by your instructor. But having said that, patches can be a great source of motivation for students, especially the kids.

Some Do Jangs have educational achievement patches for kids who are on the honor roll at school. There are tournament patches and "black belt club member" patches. Some Tae Kwon Do schools put the Korean flag on a sleeve. Others have instructor patches, American flag patches, attendance patches, patches for outstanding students, and…well, you get the idea.

Remember that only patches sanctioned by your school or federation are permitted on your uniform, and they must be placed in a specific place so everyone can be *uniform* in your school. Always ask before making any additions to the patches on your dobak.

> **Martial Arts Minute**
> While white and black are the traditional colors for martial arts uniforms, you'll see a variety of colors, especially in American tournament competitions. And Tae Kwon Do master Jhoon Rhee is credited with creating satin-looking colored uniforms for his demonstration teams.

A variety of patches.

89

When It Has a Mind of Its Own

However, like any relationship, the one you have with your uniform will at times be challenging. In such cases, make sure you are wearing something underneath. Strings will break, pants will split, and it's usually right at the time you're getting ready to showcase your finest technique like a jump double split kick. Just as you are feeling so good about your skills, the spectators are covering their mouths not to laugh at your underwear showing.

Actually an ounce of prevention is your best saving grace. Here are some tips to keep your uniform in line:

➤ Line-dry only.

➤ Okay, apartment dwellers, if you must use a dryer, don't dry it all the way. Take it out of the dryer while it's still damp and spread it over the bed.

➤ Have a professional do any mending.

➤ Use starch (especially before a tournament or testing).

We're talking about the cotton canvas uniforms here. These heavy things tend to deteriorate more quickly when you put them in the dryer. The heat causes the threads to loosen, and you know the rest. I don't know what you'll break more, your sewing needles or your nails, but save yourself a lot of frustration and have a professional or someone who sews well mend any spots and apply the patches. It is worth every penny. Finally, your secret weapon is a can of spray starch. For something so inexpensive, this magical liquid will keep your uniform extra sharp and snappy when delivering those kicks and punches.

Watch Out, Grasshopper

If you forget or lose your uniform or belt don't show up in class wearing sweat pants. Ask your instructor if you can borrow or buy a new one. Otherwise, you may not be permitted to take the class.

Watch Out, Grasshopper

Don't put your dobak in a hot washer or dryer. If it's made of cotton it'll shrink and look more like a Barbie-doll outfit than a warrior's uniform.

Tie One On

If you think Tae Kwon Do training is hard, wait until you have to learn to tie your belt. It is just another humiliating experience you will have to deal with as a new white belt. Here are the steps:

➤ Hold the belt in the middle with the ends hanging evenly.

➤ Place the middle of the belt against your belly button.

➤ Wrap it around once and bring both ends back to your front.

➤ Bring the left end up to the middle.

➤ Overlap the right end up and then tuck it behind and under both layers (this step is important because if the thing comes undone it won't just fall on the floor in the middle of a match because it is tucked under one layer).

➤ Pull both ends out, making sure they are still even.

➤ Tie a square knot by bringing the right end under and over the left.

➤ Pull both ends even and make sure the knot is in the middle.

➤ It is a matter of pride that neither end should hang lower than the other when finished.

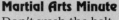

Martial Arts Minute
Don't wash the belt. Even black belts don't wash their belts after years of training. In fact, some believe that is how the black belt came to be—after years of practice the white belts of the early practitioners would turn black with dirt, and that is how the advanced students were identified.

If you can't get it, don't worry. Ask someone to help the first few times, and soon you'll be tying it as easily as you tie your shoes.

Tying the belt.

A tied belt.

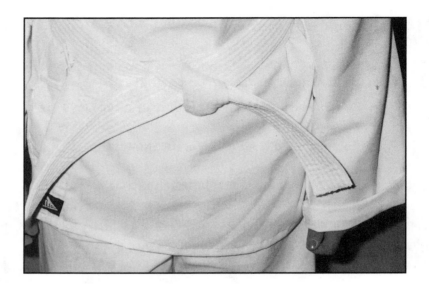

When It's Gray, Throw It Away

A black uniform often weathers to a nice soft gray. But if your white uniform is gray, then it's "that time." After a few years, even old faithful will start to look a little haggard. Here are some clues for uniform retirement:

➤ It looks like a baseball road jersey.

➤ There's a yellow stain, and it won't come out!

➤ The pants have shrunk up to the knees.

➤ It stinks, even after you wash it.

Wise Sa Bum Tells Us

It is not unheard of to split the pants of a lightweight uniform while trying some stretching or high kicking (especially if you try to keep a uniform after you have grown a little too big for it). If this happens, don't go home red-faced. Ask if there is an extra pair of pants in the Do Jang.

When it is time to get a new one, you'll want to spend the extra bucks to get a high-quality uniform. Believe me, you will get your money's worth out of it. Most people don't wear their favorite dress or shirt as much as their favorite dobak (after all you probably work out in it three times a week or more). On average, a light-weight uniform is going to run $25 to $40. A good, heavy-weight uniform will run upwards of $100. Patches and school logos on the back are, of course, extra. Look in the catalogs, but usually your best bet is from your instructor.

Sticketh Closer Than a Brother

After a while, you'll become very attached to your uniform. Trying to get away with borrowing another one is like trying to wear someone else's underwear—it just doesn't feel right. Through all those clumsy white-belt days, it was there. Through all those days you sweated in it, tested and competed in it, and at times thought you were going to go to the bathroom in it, it remained a constant and true friend.

The Least You Need to Know

➤ The Japanese term for uniform is *gi* and the Korean term is *dobak*.

➤ Uniforms are usually white (for beginners) and white or black (for black belts), but check with your school for exact variations.

➤ Patches are allowed, but only certain ones and in certain places.

➤ Line-dry your heavy uniforms and use starch when ironing.

➤ Tie your belt so that it hangs evenly.

Part 3
Making the Moves

Here are some of the basic elements of your foundational training in Tae Kwon Do. Kicks are certainly the most recognizable parts of the curriculum, but things like stances, blocks, and hand strikes are just as important. The more you understand and practice on your own, the better you'll become.

Chapter 9

Black and Blue Are for Belts: Basic Safety

In This Chapter

➤ Understanding why the martial arts are so safe

➤ Learning that protective padding is a wise investment

➤ Discovering what to do if your partner gets too aggressive

➤ Practicing a few safety and first-aid tips

Contrary to the image portrayed in many a martial arts flick, you won't get your legs broken and your arms bent backward in a normal Tae Kwon Do class. Note that word *normal*. We'll be the first to admit that there are so-called, *full-contact* schools where the order of the day is to try and knock out the other guy or girl (yes, women also do full-contact). But that is not your average Do Jang.

In fact, the martial arts are among the safest contact sports you can possibly participate in. How is that possible considering you are practicing kicking and punching to the most vulnerable areas of the human body? Easy. In all of the traditional martial arts, the ultimate goal is being able to defeat your opponent without really injuring him.

That means we train to subdue rather than maim. We control our kicks rather than let them fly with abandon. The point in sparring is to score without really hitting. In fact, if you do hit your partner accidentally you actually are penalized instead of rewarded.

Contrast that to football, for example, where the point is to knock the other guy off his feet as hard and as fast as you can. No wonder the insurance industry lists martial arts as among the safest of sports.

Three, Two, One, Contact

Let's quickly go over the different types of sport sparring in the martial arts. *Point sparring* can be divided into either no-contact or light-contact. No-contact means just that, you score points by getting close to but not actually touching the target areas. This sparring is usually for kids and for lower ranks.

Light-contact, again, is self-explanatory. You are allowed to make light contact with your opponent. That may sound dangerous, but everyone is pretty well padded up. And remember the martial arts concept of controlled technique. The vast majority of light-contact tournaments go off without even so much as a swollen lip.

Martial Arts Minute It wasn't until the early to mid-1970s that someone thought up the idea of not hitting your opponent in a competition. Up until that point there was no penalty for making contact, which, of course, meant that everyone did. Today martial arts tournaments are much safer for kids and for the average weekend warrior.

If you have seen one of those kickboxer movies you know what full-contact is like. Well, actually you don't, because in those movies the hero's friend is always killed in the ring by the bad guy who you know is going to get his due in the last 10 minutes, courtesy of the hero. But in real life full-contact tournaments, no one gets killed. Oh, they may get black eyes and maybe even knocked out for a few seconds, but the only fighters that have died after a fight (and there have been a couple) have had heart or brain conditions that no one knew about beforehand.

Our advice is to keep it light. Stay away from that full-contact stuff unless you are 18 years old and willing to look like mincemeat every day. The average Tae Kwon Do student will probably never want to get into the full-contact ring. Most people sign up for reasons of physical fitness and for self-defense.

Padding Isn't Just for Your Bed

It wasn't that long ago that all martial artists fought with bare knuckles and toes. The first set of sparring pads were clunky looking things that reminded one of a foam rubber paint bucket over each hand. But they were an immediate hit with parents. Children started signing up in droves once Mom and Dad were convinced little Susie wasn't going to get a black eye in the Do Jang.

Today pads come in all kinds of styles and colors. Helmets have been added to the original hand and foot padding. The foam rubber helmets are mainly for preventing head injury if you happen to slip and fall. Just like motorcycle helmets, some kids don't think they look cool wearing them, so the latest designs have stripes and marble-like effects to help their image.

Protective padding is required for sparring in class and in competition.

Pads are going to run you some change. It's not as bad as other sports (have you checked out the prices of hockey equipment?) but it's still an investment. Think of it, however, as an investment in your health. The money you will pay for a full set of pads will definitely be less than one trip to the doctor for a broken big toe.

Quality protective gear should last three or four years, providing you take care of your pads. Keep them clean, don't throw them in a corner, and don't let the dog get hold of them.

Teeth and Testicles

Okay, that sounds crude, but you'd better believe that those are a couple of areas you want to protect. Both mouthpieces and protective cups can be purchased in a sporting-goods store because they are required equipment in contact sports. For women, protective bras are also available. What does one look like? I think I saw Madonna wearing one in a music video, minus the tassels.

> **Watch Out, Grasshopper**
> Even though your partner may be wearing a groin cup, you should stay away from groin kicks for maximum safety. In fact, most tournaments have outlawed techniques to the groin area altogether.

Treasure Chest

Tae Kwon Do has made the use of chest protectors popular. Most other martial arts don't wear this kind of padding, but the Olympic-style Tae Kwon Do competition requires them. Actually they are kind of fun to wear because you can really feel the power of a well-placed kick both when you land one on your opponent and when your opponent lands one on you.

Safety Rules

Besides the padding, there are other things that make Tae Kwon Do safe, not the least of which are the rules of the Do Jang. Certain target areas are off limits. You can't kick to someone's knees for example. Open-handed techniques such as finger spears to the face are not allowed. The list goes on and on, so if you're not sure what is and is not acceptable, be sure to ask. Finally, it is simply not acceptable to lose your temper or to otherwise show a lack of self-control.

You are not to spar without the supervision of an instructor. That's something that kids often forget and are often reprimanded for. Be especially careful not to spar outside of class, like in your backyard. I have seen more accidents happen to those who practice on their driveway than in the Do Jang.

Relaxation for Safety

A common theme throughout this book has been to just relax and have some fun. That is hard to do if your opponent is twice your size. Tae Kwon Do is very fair in this regard because there are techniques specifically designed to handle the problem of a bigger opponent. The main thing to remember in this kind of situation is relaxation. You've got to calm down. People are much more likely to get hurt when they are tense. You have probably heard the stories of people who were asleep in the back seat of an automobile when they got into an accident. They are usually much less likely to get hurt when relaxed that way than if they brace themselves for the impact. You will have better control if you are calm than if you are as tight as a drum.

Control Thyself

What is this factor called *control*? Many people think martial artists throw their punches, but that isn't exactly so. We *place* our punches in the exact, precise spot. If we want to hit an inch from your nose, we can. If we want to just touch your nose, we can. If we want to smash your nose, we can do that too.

This concept is so critical in a Tae Kwon Do class that you'll hear the phrase, "Watch your control," almost as much as "Bow." Everyone from the smallest to the largest must learn this fundamental. The punching and kicking drills you'll do from your very first week will begin to build this skill into your art.

Eventually you will have the control of a circus knife thrower who can pitch a dozen sharp blades toward the girl spinning on the big wheel and just barely miss her head and heart.

The Big Bull Syndrome

Having said all that about the importance of control, it's almost a sure bet that you'll have at least one student who doesn't get it. It doesn't matter how many speeches the instructor may aim at him, there are two words that are not in his vocabulary—"good control."

> **Watch Out, Grasshopper**
> Control is so important that penalty push-ups are guaranteed for those who accidentally smack their partners in any kind of class exercise.

It's called "the big bull syndrome," and woe be it to you if this "big bull" is having a bad day when he's your partner. You might get away with a jammed finger, but if he is feeling a bit aggressive, you'll wish you wore your heavy-duty cup and safety glasses.

For some reason, those who possess the big bull syndrome seldom respect instructors, especially female instructors. They often talk back and second-guess every command given. The big bull tries to become a surrogate instructor with his classmates, criticizing and teaching things that are not his place to teach. He feels that some day, perhaps soon, he will be able to challenge and maybe even conquer the master himself!

But What About Right Now?

You say you don't have time to wait for the lessons of the martial arts to catch up with this guy? He's your partner today. Try these ways to keep things under control:

➤ The Yin Yang approach—The Asians have known for centuries that you can control a person's attitude by adjusting yours. If he is fighting too aggressively, you become more passive. You calm down first, and he will usually calm down also.

➤ Maintain your cool—If the Yin Yang approach doesn't seem to work, you have every right to tell him to calm down. If he is higher ranked than you, keep your cool, and talk to the instructor after class. Nobody should have to worry about going to work the next day with a black eye.

➤ The "weaker" partner—Something an instructor has to be careful who he partners up together. The big bull may not be threatened by children or women lower ranked than himself, but he could be tempted to "lock horns" with a bigger male student. Again, the instructor should stay on top of things.

➤ A "meeting of the minds"—Finally, if the instructor is getting a lot of complaints about the same student it may be time to have a serious talk. No instructor wants to lose a student, but asking one who threatens your business and your reputation to leave is sometimes the best choice.

Both men and women can be guilty of having bad control. Some have no idea that they're even losing control or hitting too hard. Usually if you just mention it, they will apologize and calm down. There is nothing wrong with trying hard and wanting to do your best, and accidents do happen. That's what the protective gear is for. After all, you didn't sign up for bowling lessons.

Funny thing is, most of the time the ones with the aggressive attitudes are the ones with the weakest self-esteem. They have to constantly try to prove themselves by being overly tough. A wise instructor and understanding fellow students can help this person over the long haul.

Watch Out, Grasshopper

Cut those toenails and fingernails too. Not only can they get torn, but they can inflict some nasty injury to others. No one wants to spar with Freddie Kruger.

Leave the Jewels in the Jewelry Box

Refrain from wearing any jewelry in class. Yes, even wedding bands can get in the way and sting when you slap someone's kick. Toes can get caught in necklaces and more than one earring has been pulled out of someone's ear in a tough match.

What If You Do Get Hit?

You aren't going to get smashed in your first lesson, maybe not even in your first year of training. But eventually, further down the training path, we all take our turns at being the cause of and the recipient of an occasional hit.

First off, be gracious about it. Unless he's the big bull of the class, your opponent didn't really mean to do it. Accept his apology and go on. And if you are the one who's guilty of popping someone's nose or lip, be sure to quickly apologize on your own. You'll want to because you'll feel terrible. In all my years of training, I've discovered I'd much rather be the one on the receiving end than the one causing someone else pain.

Actually this kind of forgiving attitude will be good for your mental survival outside the Do Jang. You can just blow off that guy who cut you off on the freeway. You won't get all bent out of shape at that sales call right in the middle of dinner. Being able to stop being a big baby and ignore a little hurt or injury, whether physical, emotional, or mental, will help make life a little easier for everyone.

First Aid

Sometimes you can't ignore an injury, however, because it is more than just a flesh wound. You have probably heard the standard first-aid advice of R-I-C-E. That stands for **Rest**, **Ice**, **Compression**, and **Elevation**. If you have a soft-tissue injury, that is, a bruise or pulled muscle, take a rest. Go sit down (ask permission first, of course).

Apply an ice pack. Your school should have one in the first-aid kit. Compress the injured area with a bandage wrap (also in the kit). Finally, elevate the injury so blood doesn't pool there.

A plain, old-fashioned first-aid kit is usually sufficient for the injuries sustained in a Karate class. That first-aid kit will have aspirin for headaches and bandages for scratches. Of course the rare but not unheard of injuries like broken fingers or knocked out teeth require the immediate care of a doctor or dentist.

Wait a Second

Some of the best advice for a stinging kick to your forearm or even for a blow to the solar plexus that knocks your wind out is to just wait a second. The pain will quickly subside and the air will come back into your lungs once the muscles relax. However, if someone's turning blue, please call 911.

These are by far the most common injuries in class. Just the momentary pain of banging your shins against the other guy's shins or having a side kick smack your elbow a little harder than you'd like can stun you for a second or two. At times like this, children are likely to cry and some adults will want to. You just can't be a big baby. Remember, this ain't bowling. Here's a great word of advice an instructor once gave me, "Nobody ever died from a busted lip."

The Least You Need to Know

➤ Buy and wear all the padding your instructor recommends.

➤ If someone gets too aggressive with you, tell the instructor.

➤ Know where the first-aid kit is in the school.

➤ Don't wear jewelry, practice your self-control, and just relax.

➤ If you get hit don't try to retaliate. Accept your partner's apology.

Chapter 10

Getting Taken to the Principles

> **In This Chapter**
>
> ➤ Understanding the principles of the martial arts
>
> ➤ Applying the principles to your everyday life
>
> ➤ Learning more than you ever thought possible

Perhaps you've seen *The Karate Kid* where Mr. Miyagi forced Daniel-San to wash and wax all of his many cars. Then he made him paint the fence. The frustrated teenager became upset because he couldn't see the underlying principle behind what his teacher was making him do. In his eyes, he was being taken advantage of. Then it all came together when Mr. Miyagi did the very memorable "wax on, wax off" scene with the young boy. Much to Daniel-San's surprise, he was learning and training his muscles to do hand-blocks through the motions of these chores.

Though it had quite a bit of Hollywood doctoring, this movie amplifies a unique quality about the martial arts such as Tae Kwon Do. Not one single move is executed without some sort of principle behind it. Every hand and foot strike—even every single finger—has a reason for why it's held in a certain position. The ancient monks weren't just making this stuff up off the tops of their bald heads!

For instance, if the hand isn't held very tightly and rigid in the knife hand blocks, you could break your hand while trying to block an attacker's punch. The same principle applies to the way you hold your fist, pull your toes back when doing a front-snap kick, or turn your hips when executing a roundhouse kick. Everything is for a reason.

The principles of the martial arts apply to not only the physical aspects of the arts but the more esoteric aspects also. Every principle, such as balance, can apply to how you stand on the mat and how you conduct yourself in every area of your life outside the Do Jang.

A Stand-Up Kinda Guy

What is the very first thing you learn when you come into the Tae Kwon Do school? You stand at attention ready to bow. This very act of standing perfectly straight and still symbolizes the principle of discipline. Imagine a row of soldiers standing at attention for minutes or even hours. Have you ever seen those British guards at Buckingham Palace? They won't look around or even smile. That is discipline!

Know the Do
Chunbi (choon-bee) is the term for the attention stance that every new student has to master. The hard part is standing perfectly still without so much as batting an eye.

If only you could have that same kind of disciplined outlook in your everyday dealings with people and problems, like the discipline not to let little things bother you but to stay totally focused on what you should be doing!

Bowing Isn't Just for the Peasants

Of course in Asia the act of bowing is to show respect. They are really big on showing respect to those in authority, to elders (like Mom and Dad), and even to contemporaries.

Watch Out, Grasshopper
You must even show respect to the Do Jang itself. If you don't bow when you enter, you'll be sure to get yelled at.

Westerners find this concept a little strange sometimes. Bowing in Tae Kwon Do class is a novelty to many, but behind the bow is an important principle of the martial arts. Respecting others and even yourself is an important element of being able to get along in society. If you have no respect for other's property, for example, you may end up being a thief. If you have no respect for other's feelings, you may end up being a jerk.

Bowing shows respect.

Be Flexible

Obviously flexibility is important in Tae Kwon Do. You have to be limber to pull off some of those high kicks we do. But flexibility is a good trait to have in other aspects as well. Are you so stiff and rigid that you can't roll with the inevitable changes of life? Let's face it, things don't always go the way we want. You've got to be able to change course and adapt to the situation. A martial artist would get killed if he or she couldn't change their approach when the situation demanded it. If someone is aggressive, you have to be able to handle it. That goes for an aggressive opponent in a match or an aggressive opponent in a personal or business situation.

Flexibility is a dynamic martial arts principle.

Power

Power is a very important principle of the martial arts. Without it your kicks and punches are useless. If you cannot generate power, an attacker will just laugh at your feeble attempts to stop him. Ah, but with the proper combination of breathing, hip motion, explosiveness...instant power.

The ability to generate power gives you immense confidence. But with the knowledge of power comes the responsibility to use it wisely. Often people with power abuse it in real life. Have you ever had a boss that was really hard to work for? One who didn't inspire loyalty but rather fear? One who made people want to quit rather than work harder for him? That is what we mean by controlling your power and using it for good rather than for bad.

Power is a by-product of martial arts training.

Learning Principles Through the Patterns

Some schools use the forms (training patterns) to teach certain principles. Again, these are principles for martial arts and for life in general. The principles behind forms are far more than you could ever imagine. These ancient moves that cause you to break a sweat just by thinking about them carry more significance than perhaps any other element in a Tae Kwon Do class. We'll go over this in more detail later.

Forms are said to create balance, a sense of peace and calmness, and confidence. As a matter of fact, one could become a highly skilled fighter just by practicing these choreographed patterns. Learning how to relax and still utilize power is one of the hardest things to master when doing forms. Ironically it's also one of the hardest things to master in life. Learning how to develop rhythm, striking at precisely the right moment, is what the original warriors had in mind when they created these patterns. Rhythm and timing is also an attribute to the everyday stresses of a *working warrior* as well. My own master instructor has often said, if you're feeling stressed, practice your forms. It looks a little wacky in front of your co-workers, but I've tried it. It works.

Jack Hwang, a famous Tae Kwon Do master from Oklahoma, has said that martial arts is about learning how not to fight by learning to fight. You see, if you have the confidence that you could win a fight, you can walk away from it without worrying about how it looks to others or how you will feel about it later. In fact, you'll feel good because you used your training to avoid a confrontation.

These students demonstrate confidence and calmness in their expressions during a form.

Wise Sa Bum Tells Us

The principles behind fighting have been blown way out of proportion in today's society, thanks, in part, to the influence of the big screen and things like pay-per-view TV. As we stated earlier in this book, fighting is instinctive; learning to control yourself isn't. It's very easy to get angry and haul off and whop your neighbor, for instance. But it hard to exercise patience and humility. Believe it or not, one of the main principles behind fighting is learning how *not to*.

Block and Counter

Tae Kwon Do includes many blocking techniques as we have already shown you. But simple blocks only prevent someone from hitting you the first time. Eventually he will strike again, and perhaps again. The ability to block and then execute a swift counter strike will end the confrontation. This block-counter combo is a vital part of the arsenal of a successful fighter. To be successful in the outside world we also need to be able to stop attacks that come our way and then neutralize any further attack. Too often people just respond to the problem without solving the cause of the problem. A counterattack will get rid of the root causes, whether they be individuals or situations.

The ability to block and counterattack is a valuable principle of Tae Kwon Do.

Give Me Patience, Now!

As you gain more martial arts experience and move up through the ranks, you will learn principles that lower belts may have a hard time attaining. One is patience. You see, to a lower belt everything is exciting. In every class, he or she learns some cool new techniques. But after a few months or years, you don't get something new each class. In fact, it might be weeks before you do anything other than just practice what you already know. At times like this you have to be patient.

A patient martial artist recognizes that skillfulness can only be learned slowly. You can't practice a kick for 30 minutes and be an expert at it. You can't play the piano like a pro after one month of lessons, and you can't experience the wisdom of years any other way than by living for years.

Relaxation

Sometimes, in spite of the instructor always yelling at you to relax, it seems like you never can. Many students just can't grasp this principle until they are very advanced, and sometimes even the black belt level is not enough to fully grasp this. You just have to get to the point where everything is so second nature to you that you no longer have to *think* about it; you can just effortlessly do it.

Obviously this has implications in your everyday life as well. If you can go through life without being so tense, without worrying so much about things you can't change anyway, you will be healthier and happier.

Wise Sa Bum Tells Us

Patience can come from meditation. Although not an integral part of modern Tae Kwon Do practice, a quiet and calm time of meditation certainly relaxes you and relieves you of the stress of the moment. Try it during the workday or any time you feel a need for relaxation and a dose of patience.

Break a Board, Learn a Principle

A person attending a martial arts demonstration watched in disbelief as one instructor busted through a stack of 12 pine boards. "That's pretty cool, but why doesn't he just use an axe?" she asked. A point well made. Why don't we just use an axe to break our boards, a gun to defend ourselves, and a psychiatrist to give us a sense of peace and calmness? We could, but we don't because it's the principle of the thing.

When it comes to board-breaking, the "oohs" and "ahhs" often heard at a demonstration are not what the actual performance is about. Board-breaking is one of the biggest boosters of self-confidence I've ever seen. I remember being horribly nervous as a yellow belt the first time I had to break a board. It was in front of a room full of Cub Scouts during one of their local meetings. I had no idea I could pull something like this off, but my instructor told me that I could do it, and I had no choice but to believe him. My heart was pounding, and I started to sweat just trying to focus and concentrate on my target. I took three deep breaths and hit it as hard as I could (a knife hand chop). I couldn't believe it when I heard the board crunch as it broke in two. I've got to tell you, my life has never been the same since.

Today, breaking a board like that is something I don't have to even think about, much less spend time trying to focus and concentrate on. It comes naturally, just like believing that you can, so you do. At my rank, trying to execute a flying-side kick over three people crouched on the floor makes me want to sweat, focus, and concentrate like I did as a yellow belt breaking that board. But it's like they say, after you've done it the first time, you'll always know that you can do it. Board-breaking in itself is a principle (self-confidence).

Finishing Principles

So what's the principle behind all of the strange etiquette you have to adhere to at the end of class? Bowing and shaking hands after sparring with someone, for instance, means that you go home with no hurt feelings. Sort of like "all's well that ends well." Bowing to your instructor at the end of class means that you respect and appreciate him in spite of the fact that he may have yelled at you.

So you see, martial arts can teach you more than you ever imagined when you first signed up for lessons. You thought you were just going to find out how to protect yourself from that bully. You even figured you might get into a little better shape. But you probably didn't dream that you would learn how to handle stress, improve your confidence and your self-discipline, and become more comfortable with your place in the world, did you?

The Least You Need to Know

➤ Every move of Tae Kwon Do reveals an underlying principle.

➤ Principles encompass not just the physical but the mental and spiritual as well.

➤ When you do forms, break boards, spar, or even just bow to your instructor, greater principles are involved.

Chapter 11

Laying the Foundation

In This Chapter

➤ Learning the importance of good balance in your training

➤ Moving with grace and power

➤ Taking a stand

➤ Blocking with your ABCs

Whether you're building a house of cards or a house of brick, you know you have to have a good foundation, or it'll all come tumbling down. Tae Kwon Do balances are kind of like that. If you don't know how to stand in the strongest possible way, you just might find yourself on your rear end in the face of an aggressive attack.

Stances and balances are the first techniques you'll learn. They are also the things most judges look at first in determining your score on either a belt promotion or in a competition. So let's put first things first and take a look at some proper Tae Kwon Do balances.

Ready—Set—Go!

The very first balance you'll learn in class actually isn't a fighting position but more of a *ready to go* position. In fact, the name of the balance, *chun-bi*, means *ready position*. Put your feet a shoulder-width apart and keep them parallel. Hold your fists in front of your belt knot with your arms slightly bent.

This is the standard pose you should take when the teacher yells "line up" for class. This is a universal pose for the *striking* martial arts. When you see photographs of Tae Kwon Do or Karate students, they are usually standing in a ready position. It is also the beginning and end of most of the training forms.

Know the Do

Although Tae Kwon Do is Korean in origin, some instructors use Japanese terms out of habit (these words have long been generic terms on the American scene) and others use practically all English.

The ready position is often held in class for several minutes while the teacher gives out instructions or pearls of wisdom. It is especially hard for kids to stand there, without moving, while the teacher talks. A six-year-old, and sometimes a 46-year-old, feels a nose itch and just can't resist the urge to reach up and scratch. You are not supposed to move while in ready position. This is one way—it's a simple one—to build up a sense of discipline in the students. In fact, some Tae Kwon Do instructors have been known to talk on for four or five minutes while the class is standing perfectly still in ready position just to teach discipline.

Ready position.

Rolling Down the Track

The forward balance, *chongul-sogi*, is the most powerful position you can take with only two feet on the ground. In chongul-sogi your front leg is bent perpendicular to the floor and your rear leg is straight to support your body if someone were to push you from the front.

You should stand with your feet apart as if you were on a railroad track. This improves your side-to-side stability. *Walking* down the track is simple. Slide your foot in a semi-circle, keeping the level of your head the same at all times. This prevents the bobbing, up-and-down motion that can give away your approach to an opponent. Forward balance can be described in one word—stability.

Know the Do
Korean terms may vary from one Tae Kwon Do school to the next. For example, *chungul-sogi* (literally *walking stance*) is called *ap-sogi* (*front stance*) in some schools.

Forward balance.

Wise Sa Bum Tells Us

Keep the level of your head even when you step. If you bounce up and down when you move forward, it's a signal to your opponent that you're coming.

Note that the center of gravity (the plus sign) remains at an even height when you step. This means you are less likely to be caught off balance if interrupted in the middle of a step.

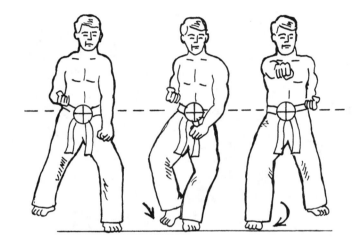

Back balance. Sixty to 70 percent of the weight is on the back foot, although you can easily shift forward and backward in this balance.

Pulling It Back

The back balance, *fugil-sogi*, may not be as stable as the forward balance, but it's certainly more mobile. Both legs are bent for quick motions. The majority of the weight rests over the rear foot so you can snap out that front leg in a devastatingly fast kick.

'Bout-face!

Remember that you want to be graceful in both stepping and turning motions. The about-face, *tuiro-tura*, is an important element in learning your basic balances.

Begin in the forward balance, then cross the back leg in a straight line behind you. Once you've established the distance, rotate your body until you are facing the opposite direction.

To turn in back stance, you merely lift your toes and pivot on your heels until you face the opposite direction. Note that your heels remain on the same line.

Watch Out, Grasshopper
When turning in either forward or back balance, be sure and keep the hands up so you don't accidentally turn into a punch or kick—ouch!

After you turn, you'll still end up in a nice wide "railroad track" forward balance.

Be sure to shift the majority of the weight from one foot to the other as you pivot.

Get on That Horse

The horse-riding balance, *kima-sogi*, is sometimes also called a *straddle balance*. Your feet should be parallel and about one and a half to two shoulder-widths apart. Tense your abdominal muscles and bring your hips forward to keep a straight spine and low center of gravity. The horse balance is especially good for punching practice.

Visualize yourself sitting on a big horse—a Clydes-dale!

Here Kitty

The cat balance, *twitpal-sogi*, (sometimes called a *tiger balance*) is specifically designed to allow you to kick out with the front leg with virtually no rocking motion to the rear. This balance resembles the back balance except that the front foot is pulled off the floor with only the ball of the foot touching.

The cat balance is a very upright balance lending itself more to kicking than to punching.

Ready to Rumble

Although we have just covered the classic Tae Kwon Do balances taught in every Do Jang and used in almost all your training forms, you must adapt your own *style* of standing to fit your own strengths and weaknesses when you actually begin to spar. Basically, you have to adjust your balance one way or the other to suit your own method of fighting and to flex with the situation at any given time.

For example, if you are fairly limber and can throw those high kicks to the head, then you probably should keep your fighting stance a little shorter. If, however,

Martial Arts Minute
Bodhidharma, the Indian "father" of the martial arts, is said to have made his fellow monks stand in a low horse balance while a stick of incense burned out—about an hour or so! Most students have a hard time squatting in a horse balance for more than a couple minutes.

your upper body is pretty strong and you still need to work on the flexibility of those leg muscles to get those kicks up, you'll probably want to stand a little wider when you fight so you can take advantage of those strong punches of yours.

The best fighting stance is a flowing stance, sometimes shifting up, sometimes down, naturally shifting and integrating with the flow of attacks and defenses during actual combat.

The fighting stance as seen head on. Notice that the hips are not squared up to the opponent because you don't want to present all your target areas and let him or her pick and choose which one to hit. Keep your chin down and your hands in tight to protect your face.

Wise Sa Bum Tells Us

In a fighting stance, keep your knees and elbows bent for that extra reserve of power which you can unleash instantly when you see an opening in your opponent's defenses.

Don't Be Unstable

Here's a principle that you would do well to memorize. Your *stability* is directly related to the position of your center of balance over your base of support. Let's define those concepts so you can see what we're talking about.

Your base of support, simply put, is the area between your feet. If your feet are close together (Illustration A), then your base of support is small. If your feet are farther apart (Illustration B), then your base of support is larger. In other words, your base of support isn't just the bottom of your feet but the area between them as well.

Your center of gravity is easy to find if you are wearing your Tae Kwon Do belt—it's your belt knot or an area about an inch and a half below your belly button.

Okay, here's that principle again. If you keep your center of gravity (that belly button point) over the exact middle of your base of support (the area between your feet), you will have excellent stability.

If however, you stand so that your center of gravity falls closer to the edge of your base of support (like leaning over your toes in Illustration C), then you are likely to fall over!

Know the Do
Keeping your center of gravity can be strenuous on the knees since your stance has to be kept relatively low. Remember, practice makes perfect.

One way to counteract this effect is to drop your center of gravity if it starts to get too far off the middle point of your base of support. In other words, if someone starts to push you backward, you drop your hips. We'll cover these principles of stability again in Chapter 13, "Just for Kicks," but suffice it to say, if you lean over too far when you try to kick, you'll end up on your rear.

Once Around the Block

Blocking (defensive maneuvers) is another fundamental of Tae Kwon Do. You should really learn to block before even you learn how to hit. In one of Chuck Norris' movies called *Sidekicks*, an old master tells a young student, "the purpose of martial arts is not hurting other people, it is keeping other people from hurting you." Of course the best way to keep others from hurting you is to run away (and that's one thing all teachers will stress), but if a confrontation is unavoidable, then you're going to have to know how to block. After all, having the best spinning back kick in the world won't help you if the other guy hits you in the jaw first.

Because most Karate and Tae Kwon Do schools are hard-style *striking* arts, most of the blocks are, in essence, defensive strikes used to stop or deflect an attacker's blows. When executing strikes, many parts of your body can be used to perform the techniques. Some things to keep in mind when blocking are:

➤ Be sure and look toward the incoming attack so you can block it.

➤ Never do a weak or slow block (your nose or ribs or groin will regret it!).

➤ If you can, use the right arm to block if your right leg is in front and vice versa (cross-body blocks are generally less effective).

➤ Tense your body at the moment of impact.

➤ Be ready to follow up with an offensive strike if needed.

Up, Down, Out, and In

Watch Out, Grasshopper

If someone is trying to hit you on top of the head with a weapon such as a club or bottle, move your head to the side at the same time you do a rising block. If you don't, the attacker's wrist is likely to bend right over your outstretched arm, and that bottle will do a number on your skull.

We're going to give you examples of just five of the many possible blocks. These basic five are used not only in Tae Kwon Do but in most other martial arts as well. Imagine a compass. You will be learning to block north, south, east, and west—or up, down, out, and in. Needless to say, balance and stability are important when you are trying to block a 200-pound guy kicking at your stomach. That's why blocking drills are always practiced in one of the basic balances you just learned.

A low block, *ahre-marki*, is used to defend from a strike to the abdomen or groin. This is the *south* direction. Begin by crossing your arms with the blocking arm on top. Step out into a forward stance while forcefully dropping the fist to the area just above your knee. The contact point is the forearm. Pull the opposite hand back to increase body twist and power.

Low block.

Rising block.

A rising block or high block, *eolgul-marki*, deflects a downward strike, the *north* direction. Raise the non-blocking arm and lower the other fist in front of the groin to protect that area. Step out in a forward balance and swing the forearm up. The fist should be high over the head to deflect the attack.

An inside-outside block, *bakat-marki*, also defends the face but from the opposite direction, the *east*. Fold the blocking fist under the opposite arm pit. Step out in a back balance or cat balance and block with the outer forearm. The palm should face you when you strike.

Inside-outside block.

Outside-inside block.

An outside-inside block, *ahn-marki*, defends the face area. Pull the blocking arm behind your head. Step out in a forward balance and block with the inner forearm. Just before impact, rotate the wrist so the palm turns toward your face. This is the block to the *west*.

Knife-hand block.

A knife-hand block, *sudo-marki*, is a variation of the outside block. It is done with an open-hand chop to facilitate a grab of the opponent's wrist or arm after you stop the incoming punch. Pull both hands over the shoulder before you step out in a back or cat balance. Block with the edge of the knife hand. Delaying wrist rotation to the last second adds to the power of this block.

Remember that we can only cover the barest essentials of blocking here. You will be taught to block with not only your arms but also your legs, knees, elbows, hips, and shoulders. Blocks can be strikes (as we've shown you here), or they can be mere deflections of an opponent's blows. Remember never to stop in the middle of an attack. You have to be in constant motion because your opponent will be. And keep those hands up. The practice routines are just that—ways to practice. In a real live street fight you must have your hands up and be prepared to keep that other guy from hurting you.

> **Know the Do**
> There are several Korean words to describe the various blocks used in different schools. Just like English, we might say either low block or down block and mean the same technique. *Hardan-marki* for *low block* and *chukyo-marki* for *high block* are a couple of those alternative terms that your school may use.

127

Wise Sa Bum Tells Us

Yelling when you block not only makes you hit a little harder but also tightens up your stomach muscles, helping to protect you, especially if the attack is directed at your mid-section. If your diaphragm is relaxed when you get hit, you'll probably get the wind knocked out of you!

The Least You Need to Know

➤ The forward balance is the "railroad track" while the back balance is the "L-shape."

➤ Turn smoothly and evenly with your hands up.

➤ A fighting stance is flexible and flowing.

➤ Keep your center of gravity over the middle of your base of support.

➤ Learn to block in the four directions of a compass.

➤ Keep your guard up in a real fight.

Chapter 12

Striking Out on Your Own

In This Chapter

➤ Discovering the proper target areas

➤ Learning the basic hand strikes—how to hit

➤ Making your hands more powerful and your strikes more devastating

➤ Putting together combination techniques

Although many people think of Tae Kwon Do as a kicking art, some of the most powerful hand strikes can be found in this martial system of fighting. Kicks are great for keeping an attacker away from you, but when he gets in close, which often happens whether you want it to or not, you have to be ready to put up those dukes. Some styles have literally hundreds of hand techniques ranging from open-hand to closed-hand to fingers, elbows, knuckles, etc.

Tae Kwon Do teaches that you only need a few basic hand strikes to successfully defend yourself. Of course, you have to be pretty good at those few techniques. Practice not only by striking in midair (like in the forms) but also by hitting a punching bag (you can get one at a sporting-goods store).

Target Practice

It is important that you hit in the right spot. A punch to the bad guy's shoulder is just going to make him mad, while a chop to the throat will put him down, maybe permanently. There are many vital points on the body—places most vulnerable to a strike. They can be divided into three categories:

➤ Primary target areas

➤ Secondary target areas

➤ Tertiary target areas

Where to Go First

The primary target areas are those spots on the body most susceptible to injury. Imagine where you could hurt someone with barely more than a finger. Wise Sa Bum says strike.

Watch Out, Grasshopper
Obviously you have to be extremely careful not only when practicing but even in a real fight. If you hit someone in a vital area out of fear or anger and end up hurting him when the situation didn't call for it, you could actually be criminally prosecuted.

The eyes are obviously a primary target—ever accidentally poke yourself in the eye? That's why it's a primary target.

The throat is another one. You could practically just flip your fingers into someone's throat and cause real pain.

The final primary target area is the groin (at least for men). One well-known martial arts champion actually had to have a testicle removed because it was crushed by a kick.

There are other areas a little more resistant to injury than the eyes but are nevertheless still pretty easily hurt, especially by a properly executed technique. These are the secondary targets. There are actually too many to name here, but the following figure lists a few of the major target areas.

Last Resorts

Finally, there are areas on the body that can be hurt with a powerful hand strike or kick but that may or may not stop an attacker in his tracks. These tertiary targets are best struck when you don't have the time or aren't in position to get to one of the primary or secondary targets. The ribs, stomach, thighs, and back are examples of tertiary targets. You should always follow up with another strike when a blow to one of these targets leads to a better opening.

Target areas.

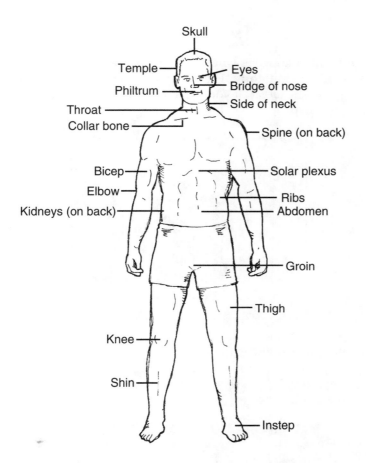

Skull

Temple — — Eyes
Philtrum — — Bridge of nose
— Side of neck
Throat —
Collar bone —
— Spine (on back)

Bicep — — Solar plexus
Elbow —
Kidneys (on back) — — Ribs
— Abdomen

— Groin

— Thigh

Knee —

Shin —

— Instep

Wise Sa Bum Tells Us

Always withdraw or snap your hand or foot back after hitting a target area. This keeps the opponent from grabbing your arm or leg. You can also then hit again with the same weapon. Forget what you see in the movies when the hero's leg is grabbed, and he flips up to kick the attacker in the face. It just doesn't work that way in real life.

In a Clench

To keep from hurting your hand or knuckles when you punch, you have to clench your fist correctly. First, fold your fingers in tightly. Then wrap your thumb over. Punches should impact at a right angle to the target. If your wrist isn't straight, you'll run the very real risk of straining or even breaking it.

Hit with the first two knuckles. The little knuckle will break if you punch something hard.

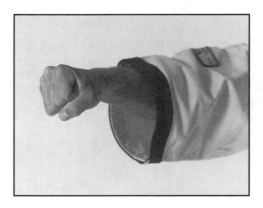

The martial arts punch rotates as it extends. This generates more torque and power. As a beginner, you will practice punching in a horse balance pulling one hand (the ready hand) back to your side as the other fist strikes. Eventually you should be able to do this exercise with considerable speed and power.

Stand in a horse balance with one arm extended.

The ready fist rotates up and comes out, and the extended fist rotates down as it comes back.

At the moment of impact, the punch literally screws itself into the target.

If I Had a Hammer

You can use the side of your fist like a hammer driving a nail. In fact, this strike is called a hammer-fist. Be careful not to hit with the pinkie finger. The striking surface is the fleshy part of the edge of your fist.

Hammer-fist.

Wise Sa Bum Tells Us

The hammer-fist is a great weapon for women because a lot of damage can be done with relatively little risk of injury to you. Many instructors show this to people taking a simple self-defense class because it can be delivered effectively with little training.

Chop-Suey

Most people have heard of the Karate chop. Well, an actual Karate or Tae Kwon Do chop is called a knife-hand strike and is used less than you might think. Still, it is an effective weapon to tight spots, like an opponent's throat. Keep your fingers together and the thumb tucked in tightly. The striking surface is a little bit to the palm side—hitting with the exact edge of your hand may cause injury to you.

Knife-hand.

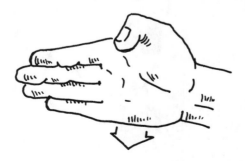

Reverse that Knife

A reverse knife-hand, sometimes called a ridgehand, hits with the inside part of the open hand. The side of the first knuckle is the striking surface. Although some brave souls actually break boards with a reverse knife-hand, most people will want to hit something softer, like the groin or throat.

Tuck the thumb in on a reverse knife-hand, or you will hit your thumb instead of the knuckle.

Palming Isn't Just for Magicians

The palm-heel strike is another weapon that is good for beginners because you're hitting with the soft part of your hand and don't risk injury to a knuckle. The heel of the palm isn't the palm itself but the bottom of the palm. The wrist and arm form a support for the strike.

Palm-heel strikes are excellent self-defense weapons.

Wise Sa Bum Tells Us

Some Tae Kwon Do practitioners develop big, rough calluses on their hands by doing everything from knuckle push-ups on sandpaper to spending hours hitting an oak tree in the forest with knife-hand strikes. Although big callused hands definitely make you look tough, they really are not needed. Sparring is done with padded gloves, and even those schools that spar without gloves usually don't permit deliberate contact.

Double Your Pleasure

Okay, we've covered some of the basic hand strikes (there are many more, but you'll have to let your instructor show them to you), but I want to briefly tell you how to make those strikes a little more effective. Actually you can as much as double your power if you know and utilize a few principles. If you cut off your arm and put it on a scale it won't weigh more than 10 or 20 pounds (depending on how big you are). Your whole body weighs considerably more.

When you think about it, it's obvious that a punch using just your arm isn't nearly as devastating as a punch with your whole body weight behind it. The problem is, most people throw themselves off balance when they try to use their whole body—and as we have already established, balance, or the lack of it, is a critical element in winning a confrontation. If you stumble while trying to punch, or worse yet, fall down, you're probably dead meat!

Remember the principle of center of gravity over base of support in the last chapter? Here's one area where that comes into play. If you lean over, putting your center near the edge of your support base (see Illustration A), then you're in danger of falling over. Not only that, the punch is actually weaker because you have little or no balance. So you accomplish the exact opposite effect of what you intended when you try to lean and swing with your whole body.

Now, make sure you understand that leaning a little bit is good. It gets you closer to the target and enables you to put some body weight behind the strike. The important thing to remember is: Don't lean too far.

Another way to use your body and increase the power in your punches is by twisting your hips. Note that in Illustration B, the puncher is much too far from the target (the bad guy's nose). But in Illustration C you can see how with a simple twist of the hips the fist makes contact. Did you notice that the feet are the exact same distance from the opponent in both illustrations? This is important because it shows how you can hit someone with maximum power and full extension without stepping first. And if you can hit quickly without stepping, your opponent doesn't even see you coming.

Illustration A: When punching, don't lean too far forward, putting your center of gravity (the plus sign) at the edge of your base of support.

Illustration B: The arm is straight, but the punch is too far away.

Wise Sa Bum Tells Us

Although sometimes you might want to try to knock down your opponent, it is probably better to punch in a snapping motion, as though you were popping a towel. This quick motion not only creates a concussion effect but also prevents someone from grabbing your outstretched arm.

*Illustration C:
Twisting the hips
gives you more
reach and energy.
This properly done
reverse punch
literally explodes
out like a coiled
spring.*

The Old One-Two

A punch with the front hand is called a jab. A punch with the back hand is a reverse punch. Put together, a high jab (to the face), low reverse punch (to the ribs) *combination* can be hard to block because you are hitting in rapid succession with two different weapons to two different targets. In fact, this is one of the most commonly seen attacks in open tournaments, and it usually scores if the combination is done quick enough. Be sure to lean forward a little, not enough to get off balance of course, on the jab. Then be sure to rotate the hips for extension and power on the coup de grace, the final reverse punch. A lot of instructors will yell at their students to do combinations when they are sparring.

A combination is literally putting more than one technique together in a row. Practically speaking, however, a Tae Kwon Do combination is a series of continually flowing strikes to varying target areas. It's really not just one-two but also three-four-five until the opponent cannot block anymore. All the while you are dodging and weaving, ducking and twisting, zigging and zagging. If that seems exhausting, it is. Watch a good boxing match and you'll see those jab/punch combinations. You want to be able to do the same thing. After all, you never know when that opponent you are facing in a street fight is an old golden gloves champion.

Watch Out, Grasshopper
Don't try to block and strike with the same hand in rapid succession. Not only do you have to be really fast to do that but you can't put a twist, and therefore your body weight, into it like you can when you block and then punch with the opposite hand.

Up Close and Personal

The last hand techniques are the elbow strikes. In many respects, elbows are more devastating than punches or chops. Because they are delivered at such range and because you can really put your shoulder behind them, elbows can dislocate someone's jaw with surprisingly little effort. Elbow strikes can come horizontally, both forward and backward (good for when someone grabs you from behind), as well as vertically, up to the chin or down to the neck or spine. Elbows are actually outlawed in competitions (except for those strongman, ultimate, full-contact affairs) because they are simply too dangerous.

Whichever direction you strike, elbows don't hit with the very point of the protruding bone but with the flat area to one side.

The Least You Need to Know

➤ Go to the primary targets first.

➤ Hit with the first two knuckles of a punch and twist your arm as it extends.

➤ Use your body for maximum power.

➤ Snap your hand techniques.

➤ Combinations must be flowing and continuous.

Chapter 13

Just for Kicks

In This Chapter

➤ Understanding why Tae Kwon Doists kick so much

➤ Kicking like the movie heroes

➤ Kicking isn't always all it's cracked up to be

Chuck Norris wheels around with a spinning back kick to knock the bad guy to the dirt with a smack of his cowboy boots. Bruce Lee kicks the broken bottle out of the opponent's hand and then sends him flying into the crowd with a sliding side kick.

Lets face it, these are the techniques that every would-be Tae Kwon Do expert dreams of doing. Kicks are what make Tae Kwon Do different from boxing or the other kinds of fighting that use only the hands. Kicks make the martial artist more effective than his streetwise but non-trained opponent. And as you already know, Tae Kwon Do is the martial art most famous for its kicks.

Why the Feet?

Your legs are longer than your arms—just look in the mirror. And if you think about it, even a short person's legs are longer than a big person's arms (maybe with the exception of a little kid against someone like Michael Jordan). Since your legs have this kind of reach advantage, it just makes sense to learn how to use them to defend yourself.

Your legs are not only longer than your arms, they're stronger too—do a hand stand against a wall and see how long it is before your arms give out. Your thigh muscles are the biggest muscles in your body, so it stands to reason that a kick is a more powerful blow than a punch. In fact, a kick has three to four times the destructive force of a punch.

Lastly, kicks enable you to attack areas of an opponent's body that he has a hard time blocking, such as the groin and the knees. Kicks to the legs not only are hard to protect against but also cause serious damage to your opponent's ability to chase you. Even women and children can successfully defend themselves with a well-placed kick.

Tae Kwon Do is known the world over for its high-level kicking.

The Korean Approach

Although many martial arts use kicks, the Korean-based styles have taken them to a higher level. For example, the typical Okinawan Karate stylist kicks low and then tries to finish the opponent off with a well-placed punch. The Japanese systems typically use bladed side kicks. Make a chop with the side of your hand. Now imagine the foot in the same position. The side of the foot forms a blade that pokes into the attacker's stomach or other target area.

Tae Kwon Do, on the other hand, uses the heel of the foot as a striking surface for its side kicks. The ankle is rolled forward and the toes and blade of the foot are pulled back out of the way to allow the heel to stick out. This makes for a more powerful striking surface and a more devastating kick than the Okinawan or Japanese styles.

Stretching the Point

Flexibility is the key to effective kicking. Some people have it naturally and some people have to work to have it. Yes, it is possible to become flexible. Maybe you'll never do full Chinese splits, but you can and will amaze yourself if you just start a program of stretching today.

> **Watch Out, Grasshopper**
> Always warm up properly and stretch out before you start kicking practice even if you are already pretty limber. Pulled muscles take a long time to heal.

There are several different types of stretching exercises. Martial artists tend to do what is called *dynamic* stretches. This is where you swing your arms or legs using the momentum to stretch your ligaments to the full range of motion.

Author Karen Eden does dynamic stretching.

Passive stretching, on the other hand, involves moving your body into a stretched position and then holding it there for several seconds or even minutes. Yoga is a good example of this type of exercise.

You may have heard that it is not wise to perform weightlifting routines for the same muscle groups every single day. The muscles need time to repair themselves between workouts. Stretching your muscles, however, can be done every day. Spend a few minutes every morning stretching not only your legs but also your arms, neck, and back. If you can't make yourself do that or if you simply don't have time in the morning, try a three-evening-a-week routine (use the nights that you don't go to the Do Jang to do a few minutes of stretching in front of the TV).

Ideally a stretching workout contains:

➤ A warm-up period, including maybe some jumping jacks and jogging in place to get the blood flowing.

➤ Specific stretches where you incorporate both dynamic and passive stretches. You can even do your kicks in slow motion here to help build muscle memory and strength.

➤ The cool down, where you gradually slow down the movements and finish with a few more slow stretches. You might want to end with a few deep breathing exercises.

Children, as you may observe, don't have to work on stretching likes most adults do. Kids are naturally more limber. Some experts even advise against a rigorous stretching program for children because their muscles and joints are still growing.

Adults have to simply spend more time on stretching than little kids. And age does play a factor in your ability to do things like touch your toes or swing your leg up over your head. But don't give up. Everyone can benefit from a regular and sensible stretching program.

Watch Out, Grasshopper

Some instructors advocate *ballistic* stretching where you bounce or jerk into position in an attempt to forcibly stretch the muscles. This has generally been frowned on by the experts in sports physiology because of the danger of pulled muscles.

Know the Do

Muscle memory is a term used to refer to the body's ability to memorize a certain physical movement. It's kind of like learning to ride a bicycle. You may not have been on a bike in years, but if you learned how to ride as a kid, you won't have trouble getting back on one and taking off down the street.

Alex Isenberg, age six, was born with major health problems that left specialists speculating whether or not he could lead a normal life. Today, like a true martial artist, he refuses to let his physical limitations inhibit him. Here he demonstrates his flexibility.

Wise Sa Bum Tells Us

Do *static* or slow stretches at the end of a workout as opposed to dynamic or fast stretches. Slow stretches can actually help relax you.

Kicking at Your Best

Here are a few pointers to keep in mind when attempting to kick an attacker:

➤ Stay balanced. Your center of gravity must stay within your base of support (we talked about this in Chapter 12, "Striking Out on Your Own"). In other words, if you lean too far one way or the other, you'll be pushed off balance when you make contact with your kick.

➤ Keep your eyes on your opponent. This is a common mistake with beginners who often close their eyes as they kick. If you look away you're likely to miss, and if you miss you could be kicked, punched, or even worse.

143

➤ Don't just use the weight of your leg to kick the opponent. Move your whole body and hips into any kick. This increases your momentum and puts everything you've got behind the kick. A trademark of the Tae Kwon Do style is hitting someone with the entire weight of the body through a dynamic side or back kick.

➤ Snap the foot back immediately to keep it from being grabbed. The snapping motion also increases the "concussion" effect of the kick. Imagine the snapping effect of a wet towel. Would the towel hurt nearly as much if you just draped the end of it over someone?

➤ The folding motion of your leg (necessary before any kick) should not give away your imminent attack. That means don't wildly swing or lift your arms before you kick. Don't lean over or twist your body until the kick is on its way. If you raise your arms and lean back before you even start to kick, your opponent *will* be able to avoid or block it.

➤ Don't forget to keep your hands up when you kick. After all, the reason you are kicking your opponent in the first place is that he's trying to beat you up! It's foolish to keep your hands at your side when some one is attempting to break your nose or knock your teeth in. Again, this is a very common mistake that beginners make when practicing. Remember that the way you practice your techniques over and over again in class is the way you will do them in a real situation when you have to rely on automatic response.

The bottom line is kicking can be a lot more effective than punching. But if you kick incorrectly or ineffectively it can get you into a lot of trouble also.

Building Strength

Yes, your leg muscles are the strongest ones in your body, but that doesn't mean that you can break a cement block with a quick side kick. You have to work up to it. Just how do you build power in those kicks? Weight training is the first thing that comes to mind.

Do leg presses and squats in the gym. Of course, get the advice of a personal trainer. You can also start jogging. But to specifically build up your muscles for kicking, there is nothing better than actually kicking. The best way to build power is to kick the heavy bag. In the old days, bags were canvas and filled with rock-hard packing. Today they make water-filled bags that more closely resemble the feel of a human body and don't almost break your foot every time you whack it. You can buy these bags and hang them in the garage for at-home workouts.

The Minuses

Before we get too far along here we have to warn you that the legs also have several disadvantages in comparison to hand strikes. First, the feet are usually slower than the hands. Sure you can train yourself to be mighty fast with those kicks, but it just makes sense that since the foot has farther to travel to kick a guy in the face or even the chest than your fist does, it's going to take a split second longer. In a real fight a split second can make a heck of a lot of difference.

Also, because most people don't use their legs in everyday activities like they do their arms and hands, kicks are initially awkward and take much, much more practice to execute correctly. You can probably reach out and touch a spot on the wall pretty easily with your fingers, but try to touch that same spot with your big toe. It takes more than a little practice. Some instructors actually have their students do things like turn on the bedroom light with their feet just to begin to coordinate their legs.

Finally, because a fighter ends up standing on just one leg (or even none in a jumping kick), balance becomes much more critical than with a simple punch or chop. If you don't kick right on the button or if the ground is wet or slippery, you could easily end up on the pavement. And as those "ultimate" fighting matches on cable TV have demonstrated, once a big guy gets you on the ground, you're in a lot of trouble.

One, Two, Three

Okay, let's cover the big three: the front, side, and roundhouse kicks. These are the first kicks that you will learn in the Do Jang. The front kick, *ap chagi*, is the easiest kick to get down. Just lift your foot to knee level in preparation. Now snap out the kick hitting with the ball of the foot (the flat area under your toes).

Retract the foot quickly to increase the powerful effect and to keep the foot from being accidentally grabbed. Although high kicks to the head are impressive and surprising to an unsuspecting opponent, lower front kicks to the groin or stomach are more practical in a real fight.

The side kick is a little more difficult to master because there are more body mechanics involved. But it is stronger than a front kick and, therefore, an important kick to learn. Start by raising the kicking foot to knee level. You must now turn your hip slightly into the target. Just as you hit with your heel, pivot your supporting foot so that it points away from the kick. This allows your hips to be rotated for maximum power and extension.

Watch Out, Grasshopper
Kick to the right target the first time. A kick to someone's rear end or shoulder, for example, will only serve to make the guy even madder at you.

Know the Do
Chagi (chaw gee) is the Korean term for *kick. Cha busigi* refers to the most powerful kicking techniques. It literally means *smashing kicks.*

Watch Out, Grasshopper
Groin kicks are not allowed in most competitions including the South Korean Olympic-style Tae Kwon Do tournaments. So don't do any kicks there in competition until you know the rules permit it.

A high front kick.

A side kick to the mid-section.

The roundhouse kick is the hardest of the three basic kicks to execute correctly. Lift your back knee up and start to pivot as you point the knee at the target. Using the twist of your hips for added power, lash out with your leg and strike with either the ball of the foot or the instep. The foot must snap back so that the *concussion* effect will maximize the impact of the kick.

Point the knee at the intended target in preparation for the roundhouse kick.

Hit with the ball of the foot in a horizontal plane.

Wise Sa Bum Tells Us

There are two impact points to choose from in a roundhouse kick—the ball of the foot or the instep. The ball of the foot is similar to hitting with your closed hand. It is a harder surface than the instep, which is more like slapping someone with your open hand. The situation will dictate which one you want to use.

Back Up Jack!

The back kick strikes straight back with the heel of the foot. It is similar to the side kick, but you'll want to kick without much twisting motion because you have to be fast if you catch someone creeping up behind you. As with all these kicks, don't forget to snap it back so he can't grab your foot.

Back kick.

Watch Out, Grasshopper

Certain kicks, like the hook kick, are hard to control. That means you must be careful not to overextend your leg and accidentally hook your training partner.

Captain Hook!

You already know that Tae Kwon Do is famous for its fancy kicks. Here is one of those high (and difficult to do) techniques. The hooking heel kick is sometimes called just a hook kick. But whatever you call it, it's a devastating foot strike. As the name implies, you hit with the back part of your heel in a hooking motion. The twist of the hips adds to the power.

A hooking heel kick hitting with the back of the heel.

Hooking through with a twist of the hips.

Jumping Jacks

Whether your name is Jack or Jill, the ability to be able to jump up and kick your opponent in the face is a real advantage, especially in competition. Jumping kicks are thought to have been developed to knock a mounted warrior off his horse in battle. Needless to say, that application doesn't come up very often these days, but it is pretty impressive to be able to jump up four, five, or even six feet in the air and break a board.

Jumping and flying kicks take a lot of training and practice, and you probably should only try them under the supervision of your instructor. Besides being hard to do, there are several things to be aware of when flying and landing. And no, you're not going to be able to do jumps like you see in those Hong Kong Kung Fu movies. I hate to tell you, but those guys jump off trampolines and ladders that are just beyond the camera range.

A jumping kick.

There are other fancy Tae Kwon Do kicks that you can learn at the Do Jang—kicks like the axe kick, jump back, jump round, jump axe, and the flying side kick.

Many styles of martial arts do not include jumping or even high kicks in their arsenals. Okinawan Karate styles, for example, are known for just kicks to the groin and knees. Many famous martial artists, Bruce Lee for one, have said that high kicks aren't that practical for real street fights. You expose your groin to a counterattack, and you increase your chances of slipping and falling. On the other hand, it can't hurt to be limber enough and coordinated enough to be able to snap out a quick kick to someone's face. You just have to know when and where to do it.

Combination Kicks

No matter how hard you practice your kicks, you have to realize that they are just going to be a little slower than hand techniques. With this in mind, you should work on your combination kicks. It is much harder to block two or three kicks coming at you in rapid-fire succession than just a single front kick or side kicks.

There are many different ways you can put your kicking techniques together into combinations. You can kick in quick succession with the same foot or you can kick with the left foot and quickly follow that up with a right foot. Sometimes instructors will have you do combination kicking drills in class just for the purpose of improving your balance and coordination.

A low kick to the groin starts off this combination.

Retract the foot.

Without putting your foot down, kick to the head.

You Need to Knee

You may not think of a knee as a kick, but in Tae Kwon Do it's called a knee-kick, and it can be pretty effective in close range. You use a knee-kick when you are too close to effectively launch a full leg kick. One of the most common mistakes beginners make is trying to kick when they are too close. You can easily end up falling off balance, and that's not something you want in a real fight. Knee-kicks are especially effective for women's self-defense where the attacker is likely to be grabbing her rather than trying to punch her.

Remember to use your hips for maximum power in a knee strike. You can even grab your opponent's arms to pull him into the strike. The target will almost always be the groin, although you might be able to knee someone in the stomach if he is short enough.

A knee-kick.

A Final Word on the Foot

Students often ask when you should or shouldn't use a particular kick. It varies, depending on your skills and on the situation. There are a few principles however. For example, the flying kicks are best left to more advanced students because it's too easy for an opponent to see you jump up and thus get out of the way.

Front kicks are great for introducing the element of surprise when fighting close because your opponent can't see the kick coming if you shoot it straight up from the floor. Roundhouse kicks, on the other hand, are better *reach kicks* because you can really extend your leg and reach the other guy.

You just need to get a feel for the right kick at the right time. After a while, you'll find that you are more comfortable with a certain kind of kick. For instance, a lot of guys prefer the roundhouse kick to the front kick, whereas a lot of female students will prefer the opposite. Some instructors say that this has to do with basic anatomy and the different hip structure of the sexes. But whatever the reason, don't use your body as an excuse not to practice a certain kick, because when you test for a belt promotion, you'll still have to do the kicks required for that level.

The Least You Need to Know

- ➤ The legs are longer and stronger than the arms and are thus more effective weapons.
- ➤ Dynamic stretching is common in the martial arts, but you should also do passive stretching to improve your flexibility.
- ➤ Snap your kicks back to improve power and to prevent the bad guy from grabbing your foot.
- ➤ There are many Tae Kwon Do kicks, but the basic three are the front, side, and roundhouse kicks.
- ➤ The knee can be also be used to kick effectively.

Chapter 14

Formulas for Perfection

In This Chapter

➤ Understanding what forms are good for

➤ Discovering the forms you need to learn

➤ Making your forms the best they can be

Forms, patterns, routines, martial arts dance steps…why do we do them? Go into any Tae Kwon Do or Karate school and you'll see the students practicing what looks like a strange series of dance moves. They spin and kick, turn and yell, sometimes they jump, and sometimes they even drop to the floor. Each system has a little different set of routines, but they all accomplish the same purpose.

Remembering the moves in the right sequence improves your memory and the ability to have the body do exactly what the mind tells it to. Of course proper stances, dynamic power, and timed breathing are all components of a well-done form. So if you practice until you can do all the moves correctly, you will develop all these aspects of your martial art and much more.

Today forms are also used as a part of the requirements you'll have to meet to pass to the next rank level. The first few forms are fairly simple with as few as a dozen steps or so. The more advanced ones can have steps numbering more than 70 or 80. (Some Chinese patterns can have literally hundreds of moves—aren't you glad you do Tae Kwon Do?)

The First Forms

Do you remember back in Chapter 2, "Digging Up the Roots of the Do," learning about Bodhidharma, the monk who developed the exercises for his sleepy companions in the 6th century? Some people say his "18 Movements" were the first martial arts routines or forms. Other people disagree and say there are patterns even older than that. Whichever is true, the very idea of practicing fighting techniques by doing pre-arranged moves in a set sequence is hundreds of years old.

Today there are hundreds of forms counting the many different styles of martial arts. Some forms are almost universal, seen in several different systems, while other schools have a totally unique set of patterns. Usually each style will have 15 to 20 different forms going from simple ones for the beginning ranks and moving up to very complicated ones for the advanced black belts. Some martial arts forms are so old their beginnings actually have legends surrounding them. Most of the Tae Kwon Do forms, however, are modern patterns designed in the last half of the 20th century.

There are at least six major sets of Tae Kwon Do forms in existence today. Some of the first modern Korean styles, like Tang Soo Do, used forms borrowed from Japanese and Okinawan Karate. In fact, if you examine the Tang Soo Do patterns, you'll find that they are almost exact replicas of Shotokan Karate forms. Some schools of Tae Kwon Do which have their early roots in Tang Soo Do still use these forms called the Pyung ahn patterns.

General Choi's original Tae Kwon Do forms had different sequences but were largely patterned after Karate forms and had many of the same moves. When Choi left South Korea, the World TKD Federation came up with the Pal Gye and later the Tae Guk patterns. The Tae Guk forms especially are actually very un-Karate–like, with high, so-called *walking stances* where the performer is practically standing straight up. Although these upright balances certainly aid with high kicks, they don't strengthen the leg muscles as much as some of the more traditional forms.

Several other sets of forms have been devised over the last decade or so. The American TKD Association, one of the larger groups in the United States, uses the Song Ahm patterns. Jhoon Rhee, the man who brought Tae Kwon Do to America, also has made up his own set of forms, which are used in his affiliated schools.

> **Know the Do**
> General Choi Hong Hi devised the first truly modern set of Tae Kwon Do forms in the late 1950s and early 1960s. They are called the Chang Hon or *blue cottage* patterns (and sometimes the Chon ji forms after the name of the first pattern in the set) and are used in the International TKD Federation and in many off-shoot schools of Tae Kwon Do.

> **Martial Arts Minute**
> Tae Kwon Do is primarily an empty-handed style, so the use of weapons forms is rare, although some schools do incorporate patterns with the staff, nunchaku, or sword. There is a whole system of martial arts devoted to just weapons training called Kobudo, or *old warrior ways*. If you remember the Ninja Turtle movies, you have seen some of these Okinawan and Japanese weapons such as the sai (short swords) and tonfa (handled baton).

Form Your Own Opinions

In Asian schools, forms practice is considered to be just as important as actual fighting practice. But believe it or not, there are some modern martial artists who say that forms are a waste of time and that students should concentrate on sparring alone. Most of the people who say that, however, are Americans (who tend to be less patient than Asians) and/or people who don't look very good doing their techniques by themselves.

Indeed, you have to be patient to learn a new form—especially the advanced ones which can have dozens of steps—and you must have coordination and some element of natural grace to make a form look good. But having said that, don't feel like you'll never be able to do a good form if you consider yourself uncoordinated. Forms are actually a great way to build your coordination.

Wise Sa Bum Tells Us

Don't get ahead of yourself. Some people want to learn several forms at once. But heed our advice and take it one step at a time. You'll confuse yourself and mix up the moves unless you learn only the forms for your next promotion.

The Art of the Martial Arts

Let's face it, if you watch some fighting competitions where people are just knocking each other's brains out, it doesn't exactly look like art. But a well-done spinning backfist or a jump hook kick can be downright beautiful. You just have to practice making it so.

Now admittedly there are some fighters who will never look pretty doing forms but who can really kick butt on the mat. By and large, though, the students who trip over themselves while trying to do their forms will also have a hard time being very good at sparring. There is an old Tae Kwon Do adage, "If you look effective doing your techniques in forms, you will be effective doing those techniques on an opponent."

And that is the bottom line for forms. You are perfecting your moves, blocks, kicks, and punches so that ultimately you will be more efficient and, yes, more beautiful, when you really have to use them on a bad guy.

A Breath of Fresh Air

Breathing is one of the critical factors in a good form. You must exhale on each defensive or offensive move. A proper martial arts breath is deep, from the abdomen. Tighten your stomach muscles in case an opponent crashes through your defenses and accidentally hits you in the mid-section. By forcefully blowing the air out of your mouth when you strike, you'll actually increase the power of that kick or punch quite a bit. That's why you see those weight lifters on TV yell out when they heave that barbell overhead. Tennis players, football players—they all exhale at the moment of impact. And in certain movements of the form, you will actually kiap (scream out in a deep and powerful manner). Don't yell on every step though, just on the ones where it is called for.

Some students sound like a choo-choo train when they are doing their forms. You want to exhale forcefully, yes, maybe even making a hissing sound, but breathe from the abdomen rather than from the mouth. One sure way to tell if you are breathing wrong is to note if your cheeks are puffing out. If they are, you are not breathing correctly.

Mirror, Mirror on the Wall

Know the Do

The Japanese word for form is *kata*. You will see kata competitions in most tournaments. That's where the contestants do their forms and are graded on their performance just like gymnastics or ice-skating. A lot of Americans just say kata when referring to forms, although technically the Koreans use the words *hyung* and *poomse*.

Many schools have full-length mirrors on the wall to aid in your forms. Keeping an eye on your own balance and watching your own kicks is certainly helpful in detecting bad form and in improving your technique. But be careful. Many a student has been guilty of staring at himself in the mirror instead of focusing on that imaginary opponent in front of him. That's one of the main lessons of forms. Imagine real and dangerous attackers that you must evade, block, and hit.

Besides looking in the mirrors to check on yourself, you can do the exact opposite and practice your forms with your eyes closed. This way you can *feel* your way through each step. Since all forms start and stop in the same direction, you should be facing the same way when you open your eyes at the end of the form. But don't do this in a crowded classroom for obvious reasons.

Relax!

When you first learn a form, you will be trying hard to remember all the steps in the right order and to perform each move the way it is supposed to be done. That can get you uptight. Well, relax. Not only will relaxing make you feel better, it will make your forms more powerful as well. That's sometimes difficult to do since the Korean systems are supposed to be *hard* styles with lots of penetrating and powerful strikes and kicks. But remember the key is to stay relaxed.

Get in the Spirit of Things

You should have a sense of *spirituality* when you do your forms. Each form begins and ends with a slow and respectful bow. Although the martial arts contain deadly strikes, the overriding philosophy is one of non-violence, which is why every pattern starts with a defensive move. You can literally feel *at one* with yourself mentally and physically when you perform a correct pattern. After completing a workout of hard, well-done forms, you can feel an amazing sense of peace and satisfaction.

Not Too Fast, Not Too Slow, but Just Right!

Timing is critical to a good martial arts form. If you do your forms too fast, they will probably be sloppy and have no distinction of technique. If you do them too slow and with hesitation, you'll look as if you forgot the proper steps. Ideally there is an ever-so-slight pause at each movement—just enough to allow the block or strike to be delivered with accurate power and focus. But this pause is very subtle. To many uneducated observers (like you were before you read this book), there is almost no pause in a form. Each step seems to follow swiftly on the heels of the previous one.

One master has said, "As each drop of water joins with the others to make a steady stream, so the individual steps of a form join to make a flowing river." As you get better, this whole idea of distinct and powerful techniques that nevertheless join together to make a rhythmic, flowing dance will become easier to do.

There are several other things to keep in mind when you do your forms:

➤ Each form should end in not only in the same direction as when you began but the same exact spot.

➤ Footwork is as important as what you do with your hands—maybe even more so.

➤ Balance must be maintained at all times, and each stance should be perfect.

Martial Arts Minute
If you look closely, you'll see some animal-like movements in the forms. In centuries past, martial arts masters would often spend years just watching the animals fight to defend their territories. Then they would devise techniques based on the most successful animal fighting moves.

Watch Out, Grasshopper
Be careful where you do your forms. Doing them in the back yard, for example, may be a great way to practice at home, but watch out for uneven ground, gopher holes, and doggie presents (you know what we mean). And if you practice out on the driveway in your slick-soled street shoes, you may end up as part of the concrete.

➤ Detail counts. Spend time on the little things like pulling your fist all the way back and hitting with the proper parts of your hands and feet.

The True Meaning

Each move of a form, of course, simulates a real block or strike. Sometimes, however, the true meaning of a particular move is much deeper than it seems at first glance. Often the instructor tells the students only the simplest explanation and reserves the more complicated meanings until later in the student's development. Unfortunately in the traditional Asian martial art way of looking at things "later" can mean five or 10 years down the road. What this means is that there are a lot of first-degree black belts running around who have never had the sophisticated applications of some techniques fully explained to them. These instructors continue to teach only the most basic applications.

Why, you may ask, do some teachers withhold certain information until they deem the student ready? Actually, this withholding of the deeper meanings of the arts has long been a tradition in Asia. Sometimes the master wishes to wait until he knows the student is ready to receive and comprehend the information. Sometimes he waits until he can trust the student with this sometimes deadly knowledge. Sometimes it is a test of the student's patience.

In ancient times, remember, there were often warring factions in the land. Techniques were carefully taught to only those in the family (in the case of family styles) or in the army of the king (in the warrior classes). Even then, sometimes the actual techniques could not be practiced openly because other factions might have sent spies to learn the favorite moves of the system. Therefore some secrets were hidden within each training routine—secrets that only a select few actually knew. What secrets? Well, a certain move that at first glance seems like a simple block, for example, might also reveal an incapacitating pressure point strike if you examine the technique more closely. See the following illustrations.

Know the Do
The whole idea of the meaning behind certain moves in the training forms is often called *bunkai*, which is the Japanese term for *application of technique*. There are whole books, videos, and seminars devoted to just this single concept of the martial arts.

Martial Arts Minute
Although other sports do routines to music, ice-skating for example, martial arts forms just recently incorporated *musical forms*. Today musical forms are a crowd favorite at most open-style tournaments.

The basic explanation. Fold...

...a simple down block.

*An advanced explanation.
A wrist grab.*

Reverse the grab.

*Strike to a pressure point on
the arm.*

Just Do It

Okay, enough talk about how to do the forms. Let's actually take a look at the beginning patterns you will be learning in your Tae Kwon Do classes. Since you may be taking one of the several different styles of Tae Kwon Do, we've included the first form of the four most frequently seen styles in North America: the Chang Hon, Tae Guk, Song Ahm, and Jhoon Rhee styles.

Chon ji

The first of these four forms to be devised was Chon ji, literally *Heaven and Earth*, a great name for the first form of a system don't you think? It was first used by General Choi Hong Hi's International TKD Federation (as the beginning pattern in his Chang Hon system) and was widely taught in the West even before the World TKD Federation was formed. Thus many schools of American Tae Kwon Do and several associations, such as the International TKD Association, the American Karate and Tae Kwon Do Organization (A-KaTo), and Tae Kwon Do Organization, still use Chon ji even though they are not affiliated with the ITF.

Chon ji.

Tae Guk

Although the World Tae Kwon Do Federation first designed the Pal Gye forms to replace the exiled Chang Hon patterns, they have since been supplanted by the newer Tae Guks. The main difference is the Tae Guks utilize the more upright walking stances of the South Korean Olympic style. Here is Tae Guk El Jong.

> **Know the Do**
> Chang Hon literally means "blue cottage," thus the blue cottage forms were the first Tae Kwon Do patterns.

Tae Guk El Jong.

Song Ahm

The American Tae Kwon Do Association is one of the larger groups in North America. They used the Chang Hon forms in their early years but have since designed their own Song Ahm, or *Pine Tree Cell* forms. This is Song Ahm pattern number one.

Song Ahm One.

Jayoo

Jhoon Rhee was the man who first introduced the West to the Korean martial arts back in mid 1950s. He originally taught the Pyung Dan forms, later changed to the Chang Hon forms, and now has designed his own set of patterns. The name of the first form, Jayoo, means *freedom*.

Jayoo.

The Least You Need to Know

➤ Different styles of Tae Kwon Do practice different forms.

➤ A form is a series of defensive and offensive techniques designed to help you perfect your various moves.

➤ Breathe on each block or strike, and yell with all your spirit.

➤ Although each step and technique should be distinct and powerful there is a *rhythm* or sense of *flow* that must be maintained.

➤ Some moves have more complicated applications that only the more advanced students will be allowed to learn.

Part 4
Putting It All Together

How can you possibly grasp everything the martial arts offer? Well, actually it takes a lifetime. That is why they call it a way of life. But you can take it slowly, one step at a time. There are so many things to ponder that you literally have to take years to realize the lessons.

That's good...
one step
is all
I can handle...

Chapter 15

One Step to Practicality: One-Step Sparring

In This Chapter

➤ Pre-arranged sparring can help your techniques

➤ Having a partner you can trust

➤ Getting as close as you can to real fighting and still staying safe

➤ Becoming an artist and creating your own one-steps

Forms and free-sparring occupy opposite ends of the spectrum. Forms are the way to learn and practice your moves by yourself, and sparring is your chance to actually try and apply the forms on an unpredictable opponent. So what's in the middle? There must be a way for the novice student to apply the empty moves in a controlled setting against an opponent before you get to the kind of free-for-all environment of the sparring match.

Well, there is such a means of training. It's called *one-step sparring*. Defined, one-steps are controlled and pre-arranged sparring against an opponent who will attack you in a precise and prescribed manner.

Actually one-steps can be really fun. You get to do all kinds of neat techniques in a setting where you can show off without fear of getting blasted by an overly aggressive attacker. That's why many instructors like to use one-steps as demonstration techniques and that's why almost all Tae Kwon Do rank examinations contain one-steps.

Taking the Step

Although the exact formal procedures of the attack may vary a little from school to school, the basic idea is that the attacker takes *one step* toward you with a punch (or sometimes a kick) and then you have to defend. In our school, the defender will yell first, signaling his or her readiness. The attacker will step back with the right foot into a forward balance and execute a downward block with the left hand as he lets out a fierce yell of his own. After a momentary pause the attacker lunges forward into a right forward balance and punches to the defender's face.

Know the Do

"Ilbo taeryon" is the Korean term for *one-step sparring*. In Japanese styles you'll hear the term "ippon kumite."

If that sounds scary, it's really not because you know exactly what to expect. A single punch to your face is the prescribed attack. This way you don't have to concentrate on anything but a well-executed defense and counterattack. Of course the attack may change later, but for now, in the beginning stages of your training, the attack is consistent and predictable.

Block, You Blockhead!

It is said in the martial arts that there are four things you can do when someone tries to punch you:

➤ Block the attack

➤ Hit the other guy first

➤ Avoid the attack by moving out of the way

➤ Get hit

We will assume that the last option is one you don't want to experience and instead concentrate on the others. The simplest solution is to block, and that is exactly what the beginning one-steps teach you. Advanced one-steps introduce the student to the concepts of avoidance and short-circuiting, or attacking first.

A common mistake that beginners make is to let the attacker extend his or her arms all the way out before blocking. Think about it for a minute. If you did that in a real fight, you would get hit! You can't allow the punch to get all the way in before you meet it with a block. (See Chapter 11, "Laying the Foundation" for some basic blocks.)

Counterattacks

The counterattacks (where you hit the guy back) are also predetermined for you. The first few one-steps will have only one or two strikes or kicks. As you move up the rank ladder, your one-step counters will have four, five, or even more techniques.

Some instructors like for you to yell on the very first counter because it surprises the attacker. Other teachers say you should yell on the final counter move because it's a way to finish him off with a bang! I guess the best solution might be to yell on both the first and the last move. What the heck, yell on everything, including the block.

Wise Sa Bum Tells Us

Naturally, the counterattack should be directed to a vital target area. There is nothing more dangerous than executing a nice block on an incoming punch and then hitting the guy back in the shoulder instead of in the stomach or some other proper target.

Size Does Matter!

Although the ads in magazines may have you believe that a little guy can take on a big guy, this is only true with a pretty good amount of skill. A bigger person simply has more reach than a smaller person.

One of the skill factors that one-steps teach you is how to make the best use of the length (or perhaps lack of length) of your arms and legs. You have to get in close to effectively strike or kick a larger opponent. One-steps give you a vehicle for practicing that kind of aggressive movement. You will learn to judge distance as you learn and practice your one-step sparring drills.

Watch Out, Grasshopper

If you know how long your legs and arms, are you can throw full-power techniques without hitting your partner. But if you are a bad judge of distance or if you over- or underestimate your own kicks and punches, you will most likely have an accident.

Control

Judging distance is what we mean by control. Needless to say, if you knock out your partner when he is just standing there in proper position, you have shown virtually no self-control. One-steps are a way to practice hitting, with both hands and feet, with full power and yet with perfect extension and control.

Eventually you will get to know your own body and will be able to know exactly where your punches and kicks are going to land. This is how a black belt can stand right in front of you and launch a driving side kick toward your face but stop it within an inch or two. He knows, from years of practice, exactly how far he has to go to hit you.

Wise Sa Bum Tells Us

Control is a term you will hear a lot in class. Basically it means being able to throw techniques without walloping your partner. There are several drills to improve this ability, but one-steps are among the best.

Taking a Stance

One of the reasons for learning and practicing one-steps is to work on your balance. It is a different feel to try and maintain balance when there is someone rushing in to knock your teeth out as opposed to just stepping into a horse balance in a training form with no one else standing there. You will be judged on your ability to stay in a stable position while you are blocking and hitting.

You would be surprised at how many beginning students stumble trying to put together their first one-steps. The secret is to stay low and keep your base of support fairly wide. If you try to stand straight up when a big opponent attacks, you are likely to fall backward when attempting to meet his offensive step. Although prescribed one-steps also have prescribed stances, the exact kind of stance you are in actually matters less than your ability to maintain a stable balance. If you fall over, you are in big trouble.

Expressing Your Attitude

One-steps are a great place to work on your attitude. Yelling and growling at an opponent in a free-sparring match may seem a little scary because you don't know exactly how he'll take it—he might just try to silence your noises. However in a one-step situation, you are supposed to yell and yell loudly. This is a prime way to show your aggressive attitude.

Watch Out, Grasshopper

Needless to say, if you are practicing with a partner, she gets a turn after you do. So if you accidentally pop her in the mouth or kick a little hard to the stomach, she gets the next shot at you. Of course we know no martial artist would try for revenge, right?

Facial expressions are also important. I have seen people doing one-steps who look like they are about to fall asleep! Put your entire spirit into it. Make a mean face. Wrinkle your nose. Grit your teeth. This is your chance to show your opponent you aren't afraid of him. In fact, you just might make him afraid of you.

By the way, this answers the question that people often ask. "If you always *pull* your kicks and punches in the martial arts, what makes you think you won't inadvertently do that in a real street fight?" The answer is that we don't pull our kicks and punches; we *place* them exactly where we want them to be.

For example, in a one-step I might throw a side kick and intentionally stop it just one inch from your chin. I'm not *holding back* with my kick, I am *controlling* it. If I want to just touch your chin, I can do that. And if I want to break your jaw, I can do that too. It is all a matter of control of my body.

A basic one-step routine. The attacker steps in with a punch while the defender does an inside block.

The first counter-attack is a backfist strike to the face.

Finish with a reverse punch to the mid-section and a yell.

173

Being Creative

At the blue belt levels and above, the student will typically have to make up his or her own one-steps. They must look powerful and smooth. They must be done with excellent balance and control. They must be effective and not done with inaccurate or wimpy techniques.

When you are making up your own one-steps, you should capitalize on your strengths and eliminate your weaknesses. For example, if you can do head-high kicks with ease, then throw in a lot of round and heel kicks to the head. If it's hard for you to get that foot above the waist, concentrate instead on groin kicks. Don't do something that will make you look uncoordinated or weak.

I have seen little kids or small women try to step in and sweep a 200-pound man off his feet. While there are certainly ways to do that, if you can't make it look smooth, don't make up a one-step where you have to do something that you physically find hard to do. That is the beauty of making up your own techniques. You can design your one-steps to make you look as good as possible. Have fun and be creative.

I can usually tell how good a student really is by looking at the one-steps that they have created. If they look crummy but the student is proud of them, that tells me volumes about their ability to recognize good techniques. On the other hand, there is nothing more inspiring that seeing a student execute some lightening-quick kicks and punches, yelling all the while at the top of her lungs, and finish by slamming the opponent to the floor and placing a final stomp into his face. Wow.

Wise Sa Bum Tells Us

Good one-steps usually consist of a strong block followed by a fairly simple counterattack consisting of three or four moves. You can do more techniques if you are advanced enough to make it look good, but remember, your goal is to show off your effectiveness, not your ability to memorize 17 moves in a row.

On to the Advanced Levels

At the brown belt stages you will probably get into three steps (where the opponent takes three steps toward you instead of just one) and even kicking one-steps (where the attacker does a front kick, for example, instead of a punch).

Naturally these require much more sophisticated blocking and avoidance skills. Remember what I said just a few pages ago? You can move out of the way of an attack instead of just blocking it. Here, in the advanced one-step routines, is where you can practice those moves where you step to the side to avoid the attacker and then execute your counter.

In addition, I mentioned hitting first at the beginning of this chapter. That is also a legitimate one-step routine. As the attacker just starts his step to come in and punch at you, launch a sliding side kick or other dynamic technique that will stop him in his tracks and prevent his punch from ever reaching you.

An advanced one-step routine. The attacker steps in with a punch while the defender does a crescent kick block.

The defender pivots into a side kick.

The attacker finishes with a round kick to the head.

175

The Least You Need to Know

➤ One-steps help perfect your balances, power, control, and techniques.

➤ Basic one-steps are fairly simple, but soon you get to make up your own, more advanced routines.

➤ Yelling and making faces can actually increase your attitude.

➤ Hit first, move, block, or get clobbered.

Ready, Set, Free-Spar!

Instructors often tell their students that *free-sparring* (where you are free to do just about whatever you want) is the closest you will actually get to a street fight without walking into a biker bar and yelling out insults. Notice I said that you are free to do *just about* anything you want. Obviously there are some rules to follow when you are sparring with other students so no one gets hurt.

But having said that, free-sparring is kind of a free-for-all where you and your opponent have no predetermined plan of attack (such as in one-steps). As in a real street fight, the roles of attacker and defender will shift back and forth. One second you'll be blocking, and a second later you'll be launching your own kicks and punches. Actually, sparring can be kind of fun.

Safety First

Let's emphasize right up front that a safe environment is perhaps the most important consideration when beginning to spar. If you're coming out of class looking like a chili burger, then you may want to reconsider training at that particular Do Jang. Sparing is not, repeat *not*, learning how to beat up people; it's learning how to stay in control during stressful situations.

When and Where?

Although you can practice forms and even one-steps in your back yard or bedroom by yourself, you'll need a larger space and a partner to practice sparring. Most teachers will caution you not to just get together with another student somewhere and start sparring. You really need a qualified instructor there with you. Besides simply controlling the pace of the match, an instructor is able to determine the skill level of the participants and their ability to spar and at what level of intensity.

You need to be responsible in order to free-spar, even with supervision. Most beginning-level students just don't have the maturity to spar by themselves without an instructor present. So you should probably save the sparring just for in-class times, at least until you are a brown or red belt.

The Sparring Stance

We covered the desired sparring stance back in Chapter 11, "Laying the Foundation," but let's go into a little more detail here. Most people like to keep their weight fairly evenly distributed while sparring. This lets you kick with either the front or back leg. You can see a subtle shifting or sometimes even bouncing back and forth in advanced fighters. This keeps the opponent guessing because he never knows if your weight is back for a front leg kick or if you leaned forward for a rear leg attack. The point is to keep him off guard by constantly moving and shifting.

Don't face your opponent straight on. The majority of your target areas are in front. It just makes sense to turn slightly and make your opponent have to come around at an angle to hit your abdomen or stomach. And if your school allows the groin as a legitimate target, you had better turn your front hip just a little to keep that area out of the direct line of fire for a quick front kick.

Keep your hands up to protect your face. Elbows are held in rather than out in order to add a little more protection to your upper body. Don't stick your chin out since that will probably be a prime target for your opponent anyway. When the other guy gets in close and begins to punch at your head (which a lot of martial artists will do), tuck in your chin slightly and even retract your head a little, kind of like a turtle. The fists are up to protect your face. Of course if you retract and duck too much, you'll get kicked in the gut while your hands are high.

More traditional martial artists will drop their center of gravity a little when they get into their sparring stance because it aids in more powerful blocks and strikes. Because the South Korean Olympic-style Tae Kwon Do doesn't allow hand strikes to the head, sparring stances are more upright and hands generally are held lower.

The bottom line here is simply to find a sparring stance that seems comfortable to you and that seems to work well for you. If you are always getting kicked in the ribs, keep your elbows in. If you are frequently getting punched in the nose, get your fists closer to your face. A little common sense goes a long way here.

Positioning

Even the *way* you face relative to your opponent can be critical. The so-called *open position* where you are both facing the same direction is great for back leg kicks such as a roundhouse to the other guy's chest. Of course that also means he or she can do the same thing to you.

The *closed position* is where you face the opposite direction. This closes off some of your target areas making it harder to reach for the opponent. Actually, it probably comes down to whether you are right- or left-handed and footed (yes, you favor one foot more than another just like your hands). If you kick with your right foot a little better, you will probably want to keep it in front even if the other guy turns his other side out. That way you always have your strongest kick ready to go. Obviously these basic principles apply much more to beginners than to advanced and experienced fighters.

Pad Up

Most schools require that beginning students, especially the kids, wear full protective gear. That means mouthpiece, gloves, boots, and helmet. Naturally groin cups for men and boys are needed (even if your school doesn't have groin kicks, there are too many accidents).

Olympic-style padding is a little different, featuring forearm and shin protectors in the place of gloves and boots.

Watch Out, Grasshopper
In open tournaments especially, there are fighters who have a boxing background and can really throw some fast and powerful punches. You can get cold-cocked quickly if your keep your hands lower than your chin level.

Martial Arts Minute
Protective padding was invented only in the mid-'70s. Until then, martial artists fought with bare knuckles and toes. In fact many of the "old timers" still think that pads are not traditional and therefore shouldn't be used at all. But they don't consider that sparring itself is not traditional. The whole concept of sport fighting for points never occurred to the ancient warriors.

Sparring pads.

If you don't wear the foam padded gloves, be sure and keep your fingers clutched tightly into a fist when blocking because they are very susceptible to injury from the force of a kick. Most of the sparring gloves on the market still allow freedom of movement of your fingers (because people often like to grab their opponent's sleeve), so even if you are wearing gloves, keep your fingers out of the way of those kicks.

Oh yeah, the arm guards and shin pads go on *under* your sleeves and pant legs. Little boys have been known to put their groin cups on right over their pants. It's picky, but it makes a lot of masters mad when you don't put your gear on right.

Bowing

A match will always start and end with a respectful bow. This shows that you are not going to try and hurt your partner but instead will show them the honor they deserve as a fellow student. Of course in the heat of battle that might seem like an empty promise, but the mere act of bowing often serves to keep tempers in check.

Wise Sa Bum Tells Us

Taking a hint from the Western-style sports like boxing or even football, martial arts competitors will often touch gloves or shake hands before the signal to fight.

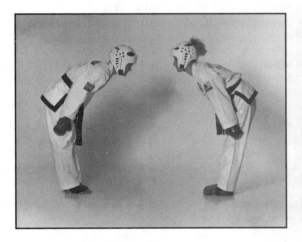

Bow to your partner.

Touch gloves or shake hands.

Assume the sparring position.

Spar.

If an instructor is present, you must bow to him or her first and at the very end of the match. Again, this shows the respect and courtesy that Tae Kwon Do students must always have. In some schools you must even bow after a good score or if the instructor stops to make a few suggestions.

Martial Arts Minute
Running and swimming are good activities to get you into cardiovascular condition. So is hitting the heavy bag in the school—this also has the advantage of perfecting your techniques for sparring.

How Long Will This Last?

In a class situation, you'll probably spar for just two or three minutes leaving time for everyone in the class to have a chance to get out on the mat. The instructor will often stop to give you and the whole class some sparring tips.

In a belt promotion exam however, you may have to spar for 10 or 15 minutes (depending on what you're testing for and how strict your school is). So you had better be in shape whenever you spar. Of course sparring itself is a great way to get into cardiovascular condition, but you still will want to add other fitness routines to your overall fitness program.

What If Someone Gets Too Rough?

Usually the instructor is right there watching you, but every once in a while he isn't. Maybe a junior instructor is running the match. Perhaps you are doing group- or line-sparring, and there isn't an instructor right next to you keeping an eye on things. For whatever reason, if you feel like someone is being a little too rough on you and the instructor isn't aware of it, you have an obligation to let him know about that fellow student. You might be saving someone from getting hurt in the future. The master can talk to or even warn that overzealous student. You can say, in a humble way of course, that you would prefer not to fight so roughly. Sometimes this is all it takes to calm down a fellow student.

Of course, if it is the instructor himself or herself that is the one being rough on you, then you have a different situation. Qualified instructors will never intentionally rough up a student. Now, maybe someone needs to be challenged a little bit physically because they have been slacking off. Other students (like the overzealous fellow mentioned above) might need to be shown what it's like to have someone come on strong. But if an instructor seems to be bullying you or some other student without reason or explanation, then perhaps you need to find another school. This would be an extremely rare situation, but I can't say it never happens.

Just Relax

Okay, let's talk about specific principles of sparring that you can start to incorporate into your very next match. One is, don't tense up. When you are uptight and stiff is when you'll get beat up (figuratively speaking). If you relax and remain calm, you'll be in much better shape to see what's going on and to block and counter more effectively.

You're probably asking, "How do I relax when I'm facing someone who's trying to kick me in the chest?" That, my friend, is the secret of the martial arts—staying calm in the face of adversity. The longer you are in Tae Kwon Do, the easier it will become. But for the beginning student, you just have to try to force yourself to relax (that even makes you more uptight doesn't it?). But if you just try to have fun and not try to prove you are the baddest dude in the school, it helps a lot.

It's Mental as Well as Physical

You may think free-sparring is mostly physical, but in reality it is more mental. How exactly? Well, the first big mental hurdle is, "How do I conquer the fear of facing an opponent (sometimes a scary opponent)?" Basically you gotta just get in there and do it! Remember that athletic shoe ad? "Just do it!"

What if you think your fighting stinks? Everybody thinks his fighting stinks at some point or other. You'll never feel like you've reached the pinnacle in fighting (and if you do, you've just proven that you haven't). Some of the greatest fighters of all time will often say that they "just got lucky." Just think though, if you can hold your own against another skilled martial artist, imagine what you can actually do to someone who has no skill at all?

I'll Have the Combo Meal

Most beginners just throw one single punch or kick at a time and then wonder why they never score. It is pretty easy to see one, long roundhouse kick making its way to the head, especially if you have to wind up with your arms and hips before you can get it going. This is the typical beginner's dilemma. It just takes so long for you to get going that the other guy seems to already know what you are going to do.

The solution to this is to throw more than one thing at a time. A lot more. This is a combination technique, often just called a "combo." Start with a jab to the face with your front hand. As he reacts to that, shoot out a reverse punch. As he's worrying about that second punch, slip in a front kick. You get the idea. More than one attack coming in rapid sequence makes it much harder to defend against. We call these moves combination techniques. Just keep kicking and punching until the instructor or referee tells you to stop. That is one of the marks of a good fighter—he never stops.

Make It a Variety Show

While we are on the subject of combinations, you should be good at several different types of attacks so you can throw combinations in unexpected sequences. Some people are known for their kicks, others for their hands. But the really good sparrers will be able to do both. Sure, you might be a little better with a certain technique, but if your opponent knows that and is expecting it you had better have a back-up plan, a technique or combination that he doesn't expect.

Start right now to build up a repertoire of kicks and punches that you feel comfortable with and can throw when the situation demands it in a sparring match.

A simple combination starts in a sparring stance.

A step over backfist makes the defender concentrate on the face attack.

A side kick is then easy to slip into the body.

Don't Send Him a Telegraph

Remember on those western TV dramas where they would send a telegraph to Dodge City announcing the arrival of the marshal in a few days? In a sparring match you can send a telegraph announcing the arrival of your kick in a few seconds. How? Most people aren't fast enough to just shoot out a technique with absolutely no warning and hit an opponent unaware.

In the martial arts, telegraphing your techniques can be as simple as dropping your hands slightly just before you kick or opening your eyes just a little before you punch. A savvy opponent is going to be able to see those little signals and will be able to stop you from landing a blow.

So what can you do? For one, try not to set up a predictable pattern. Don't bounce just before you kick. Don't nod your head before you jab. Your instructor is invaluable for helping you overcome predictability in your fighting. Of course the aforementioned combinations will go a long way toward making your opponent pay less attention to your telegraphed movements. See how it all starts to work together?

Wise Sa Bum Tells Us

Don't let the other guy set the pace of the match. If you like to spar in a calm and relaxed manner and he is a wild man, don't get wild with him. You have to be in control. You no doubt have a style you feel comfortable with already. If you allow the opponent to make you fight his style of match then he has the *home turf* advantage.

Move Around

Some people think that they have to charge in constantly in order to win a sparring match. Actually that's not the case. You just might charge right into a side kick to your ribs if you're not careful. Many times the right movement is to retreat. Don't be afraid to back up if you need to get out of the way. Lots of times the attacker will expose himself to a counterattack when he rushes in. You just have to retreat in a controlled manner and be ready to strike back when you see the opening.

Moving to the side is also a great tactic. Side-stepping is used by the most experienced fighters to avoid an incoming attack and still be in close enough to throw a punch or front leg kick.

Watch Out, Grasshopper

If you just stand in one spot, your opponent will pick you off like a duck in a shooting gallery. Move in and out and back and forth. Never let him know where you'll be next.

Think Confidently

Sure it is hard to know what to do when you first start sparring. Everything runs together in your head, and after the match you don't even remember who did what. But that will get better with time. As you become more experienced, you will increase in your confidence level. As you are more confident, you will begin to think more clearly. Or maybe if you force yourself to think about what you are doing, you will become more confident. Oh well, whichever comes first, you must learn to think and act confidently if you ever want to be a successful sparrer. This is the way to develop a positive attitude not only on the sparring mat in the Do Jang but even outside on the sidewalk.

The Least You Need to Know

➤ Always spar with padding and under the supervision of an instructor.

➤ Always show respect and follow the rules of etiquette when sparring.

➤ Use combinations and try not to give away what you are going to do.

➤ Don't just stand in one spot but move around to keep the opponent guessing.

➤ Relax and have fun.

Chapter 17

Defending Your Territory: Self-Defense

In This Chapter
➤ Avoiding a confrontation
➤ Knowing what to do if you are confronted
➤ Discovering the best Tae Kwon Do techniques for self-defense
➤ Learning the levels of self-defense
➤ Understanding the legalities of self-defense on the street

Do you think you are as safe walking down the street as your parents or grandparents were? Unless you live in a commune safely tucked away in a mountain hideout, you'd probably answer no.

Let's face it, everyone these days could use a little self-defense skills—if for no other reason than to make us feel better about going about our daily business.

The martial arts are among the best means of self-defense known to modern society. Of course there are always guns, but having a gun handy is not always an option.

Superwoman?

As a woman, I have to admit that we sometimes don't feel that we have the strength to be able to defend ourselves against a bigger male attacker. But I believe that all most women need is a little training and some practice. It might be nice to outweigh that opponent by 30 pounds, but since that's not likely to happen, women have to rely on speed, knowledge of technique, and maybe a bit on the element of surprise.

Watch Out, Grasshopper
To add to the element of surprise, you probably shouldn't wear a T-shirt that says, "I'm a martial artist." You never know when some bully might want to test your skills.

You don't have to be a super hero (whether you are a man or a woman). You just have to be able to disable an assailant momentarily so you can make your escape. And anyone, regardless of gender, or age, or strength, can do that.

A lot of people are surprised when I ask for an escort to my car late a night (even though I am a high-ranking martial artist). I can defend myself if I have to, but the bottom line is, I'll avoid a confrontation at any cost. That means taking safety precautions for myself before having to break bones on someone else.

Your Secret Weapon: Run!

Now before we get too far into self-defense principles, I want to stress that the very best self-defense is avoidance of a confrontation in the first place. All martial arts students know the first line of defense is to run if you can.

There is no shame in running away from a fight. Some of the toughest black belts I know have been able to keep out of nasty situations simply by turning and getting out of the situation. They have ultimately saved not only themselves from serious trouble but also some poor, unsuspecting aggressors from some pain and suffering.

Develop Your Sense of "Smell"

They say that women have intuition, but I have found out that all experienced martial artists have a certain ability to *smell* trouble. Have you ever been in a situation where something just doesn't feel right? Maybe it was walking down a sidewalk at night or driving home from the movies. You need to develop your instincts to read a given situation.

Here are some things to keep in mind:

➤ Be aware of your surroundings. If you are in a parking lot and suddenly there is no one else around, you should crank up your alert meter a notch. Be aware of what part of town you are driving in.

➤ Notice the body language of the person or people you are dealing with. Facial expressions and tone of voice can let you know if they are getting upset or worse.

Wise Sa Bum Tells Us

Marital artists will often sit with their backs to a wall or corner in a restaurant so they can see what is going on in the room. That way they can make a quick escape if trouble develops.

➤ Always note a way out. When you walk into a situation where you might want to get away quickly, make a mental note of where the doors are just in case.

Remember, it is always better to avoid a situation before it develops.

When Confronted

Let's say you have done everything you should and still are in a bad situation. For whatever reason, you can't just turn and run. What do you do? Try the following:

➤ Be the first to apologize, even if you have to plead weakness and say you are sorry for something you didn't do. It is better than getting into a real fight.

➤ Don't be aggressive. Often just the act of friendliness can defuse a tough situation. This is important for kids dealing with bullies at school. Showing aggressiveness back gets them into an instant fight.

➤ Give them what they want. This is especially true if they are armed. Nothing in your wallet is worth risking your life for.

Finally, try screaming, spazzing out, or whatever it takes to get attention. And heaven forbid, if you ever get into a situation where you must use your Tae Kwon Do training for self-defense, rest assured, they picked the wrong person to mess with!

If you have done everything you can to avoid the confrontation, but you still have to actually fight, don't stand around and sell tickets—get it over with as quickly as possible.

Don't Underestimate

Even if you are trained and ready, be sure to never underestimate either people or situations. If you feel uncomfortable in a certain place, it's time to leave. If someone doesn't look too threatening, don't be fooled. I know some skinny pre-teens in our school who can hit an average man in the face with a kick before he can even get his hands up to block. You never know the intent or the abilities of the person in front of (or behind) you.

Remain Centered

In a self-defense situation, you must stay calm and *centered*. Doing so will increase your awareness and your ability to escape. Staying calm will help you not to overreact to what's happening. That can be almost as bad as underreacting.

Martial Arts Minute
Many an experienced martial artist has been beaten up in a real fight because they were over-confident of their fighting abilities. Remember that sparring in the Do Jang with rules and a referee is as different as night and day when compared to a brawl in a back alley with a guy who goes to the emergency room every Saturday night for stitches from his bar fights.

By being aware, you can keep your distance from an aggressor. Don't let him get within a circle of about three feet. That is the range from which he can attack without much chance of your stopping him.

What's Your Potential?

The police have a term called *assault potential*. That refers to your level of risk of attack. You can actually reduce your potential by just being aware of a few facts. People who walk down the street, in a mall, or in a parking lot oblivious to what is happening around them have a high potential of assault. When you're not paying attention is just when a mugger or pickpocket will be there.

Try this exercise. Go to the mall and sit on a bench. Watch people walk by. Pretend you are a mugger or purse snatcher looking for a victim. Some people wander aimlessly, slowly. They don't really have any place to go and they don't seem to be paying attention to who is coming up beside them. Others walk swiftly to a definite destination. They have a confident gait and a determined glare. Now which one—you purse snatcher you—are you going to follow out to the parking lot?

Wise Sa Bum Tells Us

Most martial artists are never approached by an attacker because they tend to carry themselves differently than an untrained individual.

Home Sweet Home

This isn't a book on home security, but a few words do seem to fit in well right about now. Do you lock your doors every time you run out to the corner store? Are the windows on your house locked right now? Do you have a peep hole on your front door? Do your kids answer the door without looking through that peep hole? Do you check the ID of the package delivery man before opening the door for him? Do you leave on a few lights when you're going to be out after dark? Do you stop the paper delivery when you are going away for a couple of days?

I know; you already are aware of all these safety tips. But if you don't practice them, you might as well have never heard them. Here are some other common-sense questions to ask yourself. Do you walk right past an alleyway without looking in first? Do you check the back seat of the car before climbing in? Do you check your rear-view mirror just to see if the same car remains behind you for several miles?

Using Tae Kwon Do for Self-Defense

Initially you'll learn some basic self-defense techniques, perhaps even in your first class. These are only the most basic of moves. You must practice them, almost by the numbers, for them to begin to settle into your consciousness. Later you will learn more advanced moves, and you'll get to the point where you can even begin to improvise. But you have to start somewhere, and that's usually a slow start, so don't get discouraged.

Remember the three primary target areas of Chapter 11, "Laying the Foundation"? The eyes, throat, and groin are the best places to incapacitate an attacker with the least amount of effort. Use your finger tips to the eyes. Chop him in the throat, and knee or front kick him in the groin.

Eyes.

Throat.

Groin.

Even trained black belts could break their knuckles trying to punch someone in the head in a real fight. Instead use your palm strikes or finger tips. Don't swing your arms wildly. If the other guy has any boxing abilities whatsoever you will be at a disadvantage. And while you are thinking of kicking his groin or knees, remember he could be thinking the same thing, so protect your own vital areas.

Principles

The very same principles that you've learned for one-steps and for sparring (see Chapter 15, "One Step to Practicality: One-Step Sparring") also apply to self-defense. Stay erect and don't lean or fall forward. Maintain a stable balance. Yell when you want to increase the power of your blocks and attacks. Follow through with combinations. Breathe when you hit.

Wise Sa Bum Tells Us

A yell not only makes you hit harder but it serves to startle the attacker. You can scream loudly just a split second before you strike, taking advantage of their surprise.

Just like in sparring, the better conditioned your body the better you will perform. Use the same kind of assertive attitude that you developed in your one-step training. Be aware of proper distance and timing.

Levels of Defense

There are three levels of intensity that you can use in a real self-defense situation. Think of them as light, medium, and hard:

➤ The light technique is merely an escape where you do not injure the opponent but just get away from the attack.

➤ A medium technique is called for when the opponent persists in bothering you or wants to hurt you. The medium-type move will inflict a minimum amount of pain on him but not enough to have to call 911. These kinds of defenses will teach him a lesson, mainly not to mess with you again.

➤ The highest level of defensive techniques are the hardest and will definitely cause injury. You should only use these when your physical well-being or your life is in danger. Because you could end up hurting the other person, you need to be aware of the consequences.

A light technique to escape a bear hug attack.

Drop and extend your arms. This doesn't hurt the opponent and you are now free to run.

A medium technique to hold the attacker helpless.

Grab his hand, step back, and press over the top with your elbow.

A hard technique for when the situation is life or death.

Step to the side with an x-block.

Use his momentum to swing his arm around.

Finish with a kick.

When to Injure

Now, most responsible people don't want to hurt someone else. That is commendable, but does your attacker feel the same way? Most street punks these days don't give a second thought about your well-being. It may sound callous, but you have to be able to defend yourself and your loved ones to the best of your ability, even if it means hurting someone. Even if you have trained for years and you know the right techniques to do, it does little good if you can't actually use those techniques in a real situation because you freeze either out of fear or out of a hesitancy to injure someone else.

Get Your Hands Up

Remember that you don't want to give a bully the impression that you are ready and willing to fight. But on the other hand, you had best be prepared to block or counterattack if he makes a move on you. So what do you do? Holding your fists up in a ready position makes it look like you want to fight. Keeping them down leaves you vulnerable.

Here is the *defensive ready posture*. You are ready without making it appear you want to fight. In fact, it looks like you are begging for mercy. Just the thing to throw that bully off guard.

Martial Arts Minute
Experienced black belts can often control an attacker without injuring them severely. Unfortunately, a less-knowledgeable martial artist has to rely on techniques and target areas that will definitely stop an aggressor. When in doubt, don't hesitate—just act!

Keep your hands up as if you are saying you don't want any trouble.

In reality your hands are already up to block an attack.

You can also easily counter strike from this position.

195

Putting the Pressure On

At the advanced stages of your training you will be learning pressure points on the body. These are places where just a slight touch or pressure from your finger tips can cause pain. Usually these are nerve centers or so-called *meridian points* (just like in acupuncture or acupressure). Attacking these points on the body can be dangerous, so we are not going to go into a list of them in this text. You can ask your instructor to show you, provided you are advanced enough to understand and to use this knowledge with caution and wisdom.

Legal Questions

Watch Out, Grasshopper

As a point of law, don't continue to beat on an attacker after he has been subdued. Several people have gotten into legal trouble because they kicked an attacker after he was down and out even though they didn't start the fight themselves.

Some people ask about the legalities of using martial arts in self-defense. There isn't room here to go into all the details (and it varies from state to state), but it is a fact that you are legally entitled to defend yourself and your family and your property (within limits). For one thing, you must honestly believe that you are in danger. The law says that other reasonable people (like a jury or at least the investigating officer) must also believe that you acted rationally.

Generally, verbal threats do not constitute physical danger unless the person issuing the threats is bigger and perhaps drunk or drugged. The law typically says that you can defend yourself with equal force. That is, if he punches you, you can punch him back, but you can't pull out a knife and stab him 75 times. The equal-force test is obviously a little different for women.

The Least You Need to Know

- ➤ Anyone can be a victim of crime.
- ➤ Running away is the best defense.
- ➤ Don't underestimate a situation or person.
- ➤ Go to one of the three vital areas (eyes, throat, groin) if it is a dangerous situation.
- ➤ You can legally defend yourself if you feel you are in danger.
- ➤ Putting your hands up in feigned fear allows you to maintain a defensive posture without threatening an aggressor.
- ➤ Use light, medium, or hard defenses only in the appropriate situations.

Part 5
Climbing the Ladder: Testing for Promotions

Moving up the ladder from white belt to black belt and everything in between is one of the best ways to test your abilities and to gain a supreme sense of self-accomplishment. Learn why and how to travel the colored-belt road.

Chapter 18

Cruising Down the Beltway

In This Chapter

➤ Discovering where the belt system came from

➤ Knowing the stages of advancement in Tae Kwon Do

➤ Understanding the different colors

➤ Learning what you have to do to earn a new belt

Many people think that the martial arts had black belts and white belts and all the many colors in between way back in ancient times. The truth is that the first black belt was awarded barely over 100 years ago. The first black belt in Karate was earned in the 20th century and the first black belt in Tae Kwon Do was in the middle 1950s.

Jigoro Kano, the founder of Judo, is credited with coming up with the idea of colored belts to denote level of accomplishment. Gichin Funakoshi liked the idea so much that he incorporated it into his Shotokan Karate system (the first modern Karate style). The many different arts have different belt colors. Even Tae Kwon Do has different colors depending on the style and the individual school. One thing that is universal, however, is that you'll start out as a white belt.

White As Snow?

There are several different explanations for the color white being the beginning belt. The white belt beginner is pure and has no bad habits, no ego, nothing to hinder his or her ability to learn. Some people say that the belt is white to symbolize purity, just as brides wear white.

> **Martial Arts Minute**
> When Tae Kwon Do was brought to the United States in the mid-1950s, the colors were white, green, brown, and black, and tournaments had only those four divisions. But soon came yellow, gold, orange, purple, and red. Some say that the proliferation of colors was due to the impatience of the Americans who wanted to see visible signs of progress more rapidly.

Perhaps white stands for honor and virtue. Doctors and nurses wear white. So does the Pope. The white or colorless diamond symbolizes the promise of love and fidelity between husband and wife.

You'll also hear that the color white really isn't a color at all but the state of the white canvas before the artist puts any color on his brush and begins to paint. Therefore the white symbolizes a clean canvas.

Still other martial arts historians say that the white has no significance other than that the peasants in Okinawa and Japan often wore white and thus the belt was just a traditional mode of dress.

Whatever your view, we can assert that the white belt is considered a baby in the martial arts. You have to start somewhere and this is it. You will learn to stand, to walk, and ultimately to punch and kick (read more on this in Chapter 19, "Your Life as a White Belt").

The white belt is pure and ready to learn.

Life Is But a Stage

Although the colors may differ from school to school, they will fall into the same main categories or stages. In World Tae Kwon Do Federation schools of Olympic-style Tae Kwon Do, for example, you'll find white and yellow at the first stage, green and blue at the next, and two grades of red belt (second and first) at the advanced stage. Of course there are the black belt ranks which indicate the instructor's stage.

So there are four stages of progress in Tae Kwon Do and the other fighting arts:

➤ Beginner

➤ Intermediate

➤ Advanced

➤ Teacher

Stage One

At the very beginning of the beginner stage is, of course, white belt. But the colors yellow (sometimes called gold) and orange would also fall into this category. In many ways this is the *infancy* of your training. In fact, you will often feel like a baby just learning to talk and walk.

At this stage you are just beginning to learn how your body works, and you will be restricted to the most basic techniques. Usually you are not allowed to spar at the white-belt level because the instructors want you to learn the basics before you take the risks associated with trying them out on each other. The time to work your way through the belts of the beginning stage varies, but count on at least six to 10 months here.

Stage Two

The intermediate stage is where you grow out of *babyhood* and begin to apply some of your basic moves. You'll start to free-spar and to do some one-steps. At this level, your instructor may not give you as much attention as he did when you were a *baby*. And, of course, you are expected to no longer act like a beginner after you reach this point. You'll have to practice more on your own, both in and out of class.

Intermediate students learn how to break a pine board.

Kermit the Frog sings, "It's not easy being green." And, in fact, the green-belt level, has perhaps the highest level of dropouts in the martial arts. Your progress slows down at this point, and many a student has their patience tested at this stage. You'll work your way through green and blue belt (and, in some schools, purple belt) during another 10 or 12 months of training.

Wise Sa Bum Tells Us

Beginner tests happen fairly often and usually everyone gets to take them. In the intermediate stages your progress will slow down. If you don't get to test along with some of your contemporaries, don't get discouraged and quit as some people do. Just keep going at your own pace.

Stage Three

The advanced stage is almost like adolescence. As a teenager you are given more responsibility, but you also have to assume more responsibility. Once you become a senior-ranked member of the Do Jang (this is around red or brown belt), you are expected to not only perform at a certain level but also help out both in and out of class. It may be helping to teach a new move to someone lower-ranked, or it may be to clean up after a test. Whatever you do, it will be as a role model to the younger students.

If you think it's really cool to be a senior-ranked member of the Do Jang, keep in mind that there is more responsibility than at the lower levels. More is expected of senior members, and believe me, they get yelled at a lot more! It's like a family. If you're the oldest sibling, you know that often you are responsible for the actions of your younger brothers or sisters. Ever remember hearing, "You are older, so you should have known better!"?

If your little brother and you get caught messing up, you may be the one on the receiving end of the discipline because you *knew better* and should have stopped him or at least warned him. The martial arts system is also set up this way. If you are the older brother or sister, you cannot turn your head when one of the younger ones is making an error. We're not talking about going on a power trip and yelling at everybody but about having genuine love and concern in your heart for somebody who doesn't yet know any better. I'll never forget the time I watched a white belt walk across the Do Jang floor with his shoes on. My instructor stopped him and kindly reminded him to take his shoes off. Then he yelled at me for five minutes because I witnessed the error and didn't do anything about it.

It should have taken you one and a half or two years to make it to the advanced rank stage. It'll take you another two years or so to work your way through the brown and red belt ranks. Remember, you won't be testing every three or four months but every 10 or 12 months now.

Watch Out, Grasshopper
It is considered a big no-no to teach anything to someone lower-ranked than yourself without first getting the permission of the instructor.

Know the Do
Ti (also pronounced dee) is the Korean term for *belt*. Always take care of your belt, never throwing it on the floor. Fold it rather than roll it so it won't hang around you with a big curve like a handlebar mustache.

Martial Arts Minute
Of course everyone wants to know, "How long until I make black belt?" That is just too hard of a question to answer because every Do Jang and every instructor has different requirements. We can say that it should take several years and it should involve a substantial amount of work. Most systems of martial arts in America today require three to six years of training.

Advanced students should help each other learn and practice their techniques.

Weapons training is usually reserved for brown, red, and black belts.

Stage Four

Some people think of black belts as experts, however those of us who have achieved that know better. A black belt *is* a teacher, one who has the responsibility of passing on the art to those junior students, either by teaching or setting a good example. At this stage, Tae Kwon Do becomes much more mental than you could ever imagine, not only because of the added skills and techniques, but because of the increased responsibility you have as an instructor and role model.

A Rainbow of Belt Colors

Just to remind you, different schools have different systems of rank colors. But having said that let's describe each of the belt hues and what they might mean. We say might because, again, different schools attribute different meanings to each color.

If white is a clean slate, then yellow and orange might indicate the colors of the sun. The sun gives light to encourage growth and signifies the early stages of your growth in the martial arts. Green is the color of that early growth as the little sprouts peak their tiny leaves upward. They reach up to the sky, which is blue, symbolizing the wide-open space of potential.

You experience rapid growth in the early stages of your training (the beginning and intermediate levels), but soon that growth slows and you have to work harder for it. Brown is symbolic of getting back *to the soil*. Here you have to work and till the soil of the arts to dig out the riches of knowledge that you will need to move up to the next level.

Red is the sign of heat. The heat you feel will be the pressure of preparing for black belt, the ultimate goal of the beginner. Red can also signify danger—red flashing lights or a stop sign. A red belt has enough knowledge to hurt someone but sometimes not enough wisdom to use her skills wisely. You can also think of a red valentine showing your love and dedication to the martial arts and that commitment to make black belt.

Finally of course, comes black. If you know anything about painting, you know that if you combine all the colors together—yellow, green, blue, brown, red—you will get black. Black is the combined knowledge of all the lower levels.

Martial Arts Minute
Yellow is a color of great significance in Eastern culture. The Buddist monk's robes are yellow. So is the imperial color of China—in fact the door to the imperial household was called the *yellow door*. Green Tara is a goddess in Tibetan Buddhism who is called the green mother of Budda. Black is a color of mystery in Asia—black stones and moonless nights.

Climbing that Ladder

Okay, how do you get through all those colors and earn a black belt? You take performance tests. We'll cover the testing procedures more in Chapter 21, "Testing...One, Two, Three," but for now let's just say that you will have to study and practice and earn each belt along the way. You'll test before your instructor and sometimes before a whole board of examiners. Sounds scary, but you are taking the martial arts in order to face your fears aren't you?

Also keep in mind your instructor cannot hold your hand all the way until you are a black belt. He is there to guide you, but it is you who must take the initiative to improve and grow along the way. If he doesn't seem to constantly encourage you after a certain point, it doesn't mean that you aren't doing well. In fact it may mean that you are doing so well that he has the confidence that you're able to handle the rigors of training with little guidance at this point.

> **? Watch Out, Grasshopper**
>
> After you pass to a new belt color don't toss your old belt aside after putting on the new one. This shows a disrespect for what you have already learned. Instead, fold it neatly and place it at your left side.

A belt exam can be intimidating but rewarding.

Double Your Pleasure?

Double promotions (skipping a belt rank) are rare, but they are possible in some schools. When can you ask to be considered for a double promotion? When you've been diagnosed with a terminal disease, and you only have six months to live. When you're due to leave for federal prison in three months. All kidding aside, you probably shouldn't ask because it is considered a sign of disrespect.

However, often an instructor will approach a student about double-testing. I personally double-tested when I was a green belt because I was switching jobs and planning to relocate. I actually regret doing that now because I had too much to learn in too short a time. During the test, I kept having the feeling that everyone else was performing better than me because they had more time to learn and practice the techniques.

The true sign of a beginner is a student who is always bugging the instructor to double-test. Don't worry about other students who may have started before you. Don't worry about the time requirements on that wall chart. Worry only about yourself and your physical and mental preparation for that next color.

Who's Who

We have already touched on this subject but it would do well to remind you that the Tae Kwon Do class is run like the military. Sergeants say "sir" to captains and captains say "sir" to majors who say "sir" to generals and, well, you get the idea. There is a strict sense of hierarchy in the Do Jang. Always treat those of a higher rank with respect. That means bowing and saying "sir" or "ma'am."

Some people (usually the egotistical ones) have a problem with bowing to someone they can outperform. Sure, there are yellow belts who can beat up some green belts and there are blue belts who could probably take on a red belt successfully, but that is beside the point. You are not honoring the toughest dude in class; you are showing respect to those who have trained longer than you and have earned the rank above yours.

The Least You Need to Know

➤ Colored belts are a fairly recent development to signify your progress in the martial arts.

➤ There are four stages of progress—beginner, intermediate, advanced, and teacher.

➤ White belt symbolizes an empty canvas and black belt the culmination of all the lower belt knowledge.

➤ You'll have to take tests to move through the ranks, every two or three months at first and slowing down to every 10 or 12 months at the advanced levels.

Chapter 19

Your Life as a White Belt

In This Chapter

➤ Learning patience as you begin your martial arts journey

➤ Getting into the swing of things at the Do Jang

➤ Understanding why basics are so important

➤ Preparing and testing for the step beyond white belt

On the martial arts journey we must all start out as white belts. We all felt like a big ol' dorky, clumsy ox. That's why you'll notice that no one will pick on or laugh at you just because you're at the lowest rank. We've all been there and done that. Even though you may feel like a clumsy idiot, understand this—by taking this first step to train, you are going to learn how to master yourself. That's more than the average person will ever have the guts to do.

Of course you realize that the white belt is only the beginning. How do you survive when you know you've got such a long road ahead of you? You don't think about the long road at all. You simply take your training one day at a time. Your biggest challenge over the next several weeks or months that you will be a white belt will not be the first balance or first kick or even breaking your first board; it will be staying committed to the task at hand. It will be coming to class when you are too tired or have too many other things to do. That is the greatest challenge facing the white belt.

Don't Quit Before You Start

When I look back, only one other classmate besides myself has kept up with his training since we started as a group of white belts. From white belt to black belt, I must have literally trained with hundreds who have come and gone. A large percentage of them, unbelievably, quit while still at the white belt level.

Here's what you need to know to start out. You may get frustrated and even mad at times (mainly at yourself), but don't give up. If you don't understand something—ask. If you can't get a certain move down—just keep trying. If someone should criticize you or offend you in class—ignore it. Don't let that one person's misguided attitude cause you to miss out on a life-changing experience.

If it seems too hard—it'll get easier. If it seems boring—it will become more fun once you get the basics down. If it seems too structured and rigid—congratulations, you've found the right kind of school.

Taking Baby Steps

Some people are perfectionists. Striving for perfection is a good thing as long as it doesn't depress you when you can't achieve it all at once. So don't be so too hard on yourself. In many ways taking martial arts is like life when you were a baby. Someone had to guide you and teach you how to walk and talk.

It's the same thing in Tae Kwon Do; you have to learn from the very beginning how to stand, how to step, even how to breathe. Don't think about hot fries and a cold Bud when you're still being spoon-fed baby food! Learn to be satisfied with the little things you'll be learning. The fancy stuff will come later.

Wise Sa Bum Tells Us

Although at the more advanced stages you won't want to watch and copy other students, at the white belt level it is perfectly understandable and acceptable. Most schools place the more advanced students to the beginner's right for just this reason.

Patience Is a Virtue

Some instructors intentionally go slowly as they teach new white belts the basic moves. Part of that is making sure the student understands, but there is often something else going on. There is an old story of the young man who went up to a master and asked how long it would take him to become a master himself. The old man replied, "10 years."

"But that is so long," the youngster lamented. "How about if I train for several hours every single day, then how long before I can become a master?" Without hesitation the old teacher said, "15 years."

"No, you must have misunderstood," the eager young man replies. "I will train all of my waking hours. I will eat and breathe my martial arts. How long to become a master?" Without so much as a smile the old man said, "Then it will take 20 years."

Disappointed, the young man left to find someone else who could turn him into a master. The moral is, take it slowly and concentrate on learning just the things laid out in front of you for today. The harder you try to make it, the longer it will actually take.

The Mental Challenge

A lot of your sweat as a white belt will actually be from mental concentration alone. Remember when you were first learning how to drive? Remember how hard you concentrated and gripped the wheel? But today, you don't even think about driving; you just somehow *automatically* do it. Your Tae Kwon Do training is just like this. After a while, those difficult moves will become second nature.

There will be a lot of strange new etiquette to absorb too. It may seem like you won't be able to memorize all the rules. Don't worry about it and don't question these things either. It's been this way for hundreds of years, and no one is going to change the customs and etiquette just to please you. It will help if you review Chapter 7, "Fright Night: Your First Class," on your first class night if you haven't yet had your first class.

Watch Out, Grasshopper
An unwritten rule for white belts is, "Don't question your instructor." The white belt who always has to ask "Why" before doing anything will immediately find himself at odds with the teachers. Just be quiet and do what you're told.

How Often Should You Attend?

Eventually you will settle into a two- or three-times-a-week schedule. However, avoid the dangers of going so many times a week that you suffer burn-out or overload. Normally this is not a problem when you're still a white belt because is still so new to you.

We will say, however, that you shouldn't try to learn the yellow belt stuff while you are white belt. That only serves to confuse and frustrate. Be satisfied with just getting the white belt material down. There is plenty of time to learn the rest.

Know the Do
Paek Te is the white belt. In the early days of Tae Kwon Do, there were only four colors: white, green, brown, and black.

Martial Arts Minute
If you are coming into Tae Kwon Do from another martial art you will more than likely have to start over again as a white belt. If you keep a good attitude about starting over you may advance more quickly.

What You'll Be Learning

Almost everything you'll learn in your first month or two will be extremely basic. And it has to be that way. Many students want to learn how to do flying kicks and shoulder throws just like in the movies. Sorry, but it will take you years before you perfect those kinds of techniques.

Fortunately, most schools will start you off in private lessons. This will be very informal one-on-one with the trainer. And you'll go over everything from how to stand to how to scream. Once your teacher feels you're ready (usually after three or four lessons), you'll move on to group class.

Sometimes kids have an easier time learning because they are used to school lessons.

When Do I Get to Learn Self-Defense?

Most people sign up for martial arts lessons for purposes of self-defense, so a wise instructor will show you something on your very first class if for no other reason that to let you know you have picked the right activity. Although your introduction to self-defense will be basic and slow, you should practice with as much effort as if you were learning *death blows*.

Eventually you will progress to techniques that can severely injure an attacker, and your instructor will want to know that you are responsible enough to handle that kind of knowledge. You start by impressing your instructor with your seriousness while you are still a white belt.

A typical white belt self-defense technique is done from a wrist grab.

Twist your hand out by circling toward the attacker's thumb.

Testing Out of White-Belt Level

Most people, kids especially, want to get that white belt off their waist as soon as possible. In most schools that could be as soon as a month or two. Some instructors use a striping system that allows you to perform a few basic techniques for your yellow stripe. Other Do Jangs just let you test for a full yellow belt. Whichever you may be testing for, this is a big day. Your first Tae Kwon Do test!

Martial Arts Minute
When you do pass to the yellow belt level, save your white belt. Many students hang all their belts on the wall all the way up to black belt.

For most people, testing for your first colored belt is as memorable as the test for black belt. You'll no doubt be nervous, but being able to face that fear and still perform is one of the benefits of training.

Can You Fail?

Just between you and me, it is nearly impossible to flunk your very first test. Most instructors understand that you are nervous and have not been training very long. After a few months or years, though, the tests will get harder, but for right now you are just taking those baby steps. And building your self-confidence is very important.

Moving up through the ranks is fun and rewarding.

The Least You Need to Know

➤ Be patient, listen to the instructor, and just try your best.

➤ You'll learn very basic balances, kicks, and self-defense for the first couple of months.

➤ Your first belt promotion test will be kind of frightening, but unless you *really* screw up, you should pass with no problem.

Chapter 20

The Truth About Black Belts

In This Chapter

➤ Understanding what a black belt is

➤ Earning a black belt

➤ Finding out if all black belts are qualified teachers

➤ Determining who's a *master*

I have been to black belt ceremonies and have seen some people who've trained for years cry like babies when they finally get that black piece of cloth around their waist. I have also seen dignitaries and VIPs awarded *honorary* black belts and later just toss them in corner somewhere. Real black belts cringe at this (the throwing of a black belt in a corner, not the awarding of honorary black belts—although that makes some martial artists cringe too). You see, there's a lot of sweat, blood, jammed fingers, bruised shins, and sore muscles that go into earning a black belt.

When people ask me, I warn them about falling for some accelerated six-month black belt course. You are only cheating yourself by looking for some sort of shortcut. Truthfully, anyone can just order a black belt from the back of a magazine. It would be simple to just wrap one around your waist and start kicking and punching. But a real black belt isn't just about your physical skills—your body—it's involves your mental skills, too—your head. You might be able to kick higher than anyone else in class and punch harder than Superman, but you'll never have the peace of mind and the confidence that earning your black belt legitimately will produce.

Do You Look the Part?

Just what does a real black belt look like anyway? Jean Claude Van Damme (wishful thinking)? Actually, anyone who has been in the martial arts for very long knows that there isn't a clear-cut answer to that one. Go to any Tae Kwon Do school, and the black belts are tall and short, male and female, Asian, Caucasian, African-American, young and old, skinny or not-so-skinny. In other words, a black belt can look like anyone!

If you can't tell the black belt by his or her appearance, how about by their behavior or attitude? Yes, there should be something different about the way a black belt carries himself or herself. He should have poise even in stressful situations. She should be able to control her temper and be a calming influence on others. He should be disciplined in not only large areas of life, but in the small ones as well. Her sense of self-worth and self-confidence shows in the way she talks and even walks.

> **Martial Arts Minute**
> Black belts do not have to register their hands with the police as lethal weapons. They do not have to warn someone that they are a black belt before they can defend themselves. They could, however, be held to a different standard in a court of law if they used their knowledge of the martial arts in an inappropriate manner (like breaking the neck of an unarmed man or kicking someone when he was on the ground).

Sometimes you can tell the black belts as they get out of their cars in the parking lot before they even go into the Do Jang. They walk with a kind of self-confidence. A gait of assurance. The good news is you don't have to wait until you are a black belt to begin to realize some of these very real advantages of martial arts training. Even the intermediate student should begin to see improvement in these areas as he trains. Within a few years, these characteristics should become a natural part of your temperament.

So I can't tell you that a black belt should be a muscular Asian. He may be a stocky white guy with glasses, or maybe she is a slender Hispanic woman. But the black belt has a humility that is evident to all who know him. He should have the perseverance to face difficult circumstances in the Do Jang and outside of it. The black belt should always be in control of him- or herself. Finally, he should be a success in other areas of life outside the martial arts.

Okay, maybe you'll never have a body like Jean Claude Van Damme or Bruce Lee—but you can start acting like a martial artist today, and perhaps someday somebody will tell you that you walk or talk or act like a black belt. It's the ultimate compliment.

Author Karen Eden receives her black belt from Master C.S Kim in Pittsburg in 1993.

What About Black Belt Certification?

I have already told you that in spite of the fact that there are several large Tae Kwon Do organizations around, none of them is necessarily the "one and only." And besides that, the more important thing is the ability of the instructor to communicate to the students and teach them. Having said that, however, there needs to be some way to verify that that person didn't just go buy that black piece of cloth at the martial arts store and start wearing it.

If you look through the magazines, you will come across those ads that proclaim "Instant International Rank Recognition," "Under-ranked for your experience? Send us a resume" (and a couple hundred dollars, I might add). One organization also offers courses through the mail in "oriental medicine." (I'd sure go to a doctor who learned his craft through the mail, wouldn't you?)

And just who *recognizes* these certificates? Every legitimate black belt knows that a certificate is just a piece of paper. Only beginners are impressed by 9-by-14 parchments with oriental characters. Well, I could go on, but you get the idea. There is a lot of confusion about just what constitutes a *real* black belt.

Know the Do

Speaking of Grandmasters, what is one anyway? In the Korean arts a person is usually considered a master at fourth- or fifth-degree black belt and a Grandmaster at seventh- or eighth-degree. The Koreans don't award licenses like the Japanese styles do. Examples of Japanese teaching licenses and titles are *Shihan* (she han) and *Soke* (so kah).

Some authentic black belt certificates.

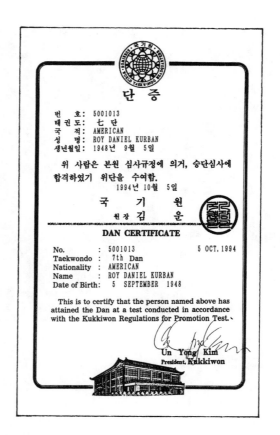

There's nothing wrong with small martial arts organizations promoting their own people under standards they have set up for themselves. Some of the most respected names in the arts head up their own organizations and do their own promotions. But it is disturbing that prospective students can read the magazines and see how anyone with a first-class stamp and the nerve to put black belt on an application form can get an official-looking certificate to hang on their wall.

Also don't be mislead by the bigger organizations that try to give the impression that they are the only official certifying body for Tae Kwon Do, or Karate, or whatever. Though belonging to a federation or brotherhood has its advantages, some of the best martial artists of all time weren't members of any organization at all!

The best solution for this confusion is for martial artists everywhere to stress that true skill and the ability to teach cannot be measured solely by certificates hanging on a wall. The head instructor at my school started his own school as a red belt.

While rank—especially a black belt rank—has its place, it should not be your goal-to-end-all-goals in martial arts study. Your goal is self-improvement. That includes not only physical skills but mental ones. Try for the next higher belt to be sure, but strive to attain the maturity and the confidence that the belt symbolizes.

Co-author Keith Yates (left) receives his ninth-degree black belt from Grandmaster James Toney in 1998.

Moving to the Big Screen

Many people dream of making it big in the movies and see martial arts as an avenue to do that. Maybe that's why there are more martial arts schools in California per capita than in any other state. Hollywood resumes are full of black belts hoping to appear on the silver screen. Many stars are featured on the talk shows as Karate or Kung Fu or Tae Kwon Do experts, and to that we say "good luck."

But hopefully these people don't realize that someday, no matter how many martial arts movies they make or how many trophies they win, they will be too old to do flying side kicks and too fragile to break six-foot blocks of ice. When the body can no longer perform at the level it used to, the mind can be just as sharp, maybe even sharper—if, and this is a big if, they took their martial arts training seriously and developed a black belt mind-set.

This mind-set is also one of respect, both for others and for yourself. If you respect yourself, you won't poison your body and your mind with negative things like drugs or negative thinking. When you respect yourself, it is easier to respect other people and, in fact, all other things around you.

If you make it as far as black belt level, you'll find that just the act of putting it around your waist gives you a different mind-set. It seems to have some sort of magic effect on you. Because you feel different, you'll actually do things differently too. You will find yourself doing all those techniques that you once thought were so impossible. Whether it's a spinning back kick or a double split kick board break, you will finally see how the years of training and patience have paid off.

Something else happens to you in class too. You will recognize you are being watched just as you used to watch your black belt seniors. Students, especially the children, will want to be like you, not only in class but out of it as well. In one sense, you might as well put on a clerical collar. Your students are looking to you to set an example for them to follow. You have become a kind of super hero to them and they are watching your every move, whether it be on the mat or at the mall.

> **Martial Arts Minute**
> There is a story that has been circulating around the martial arts for years that says the white belts of the kimonos of the early practitioners would turn black over time with age and dirt, and that is how the black belt came to be known as the teacher's rank.

> **Watch Out, Grasshopper**
> Asking a black belt to spar is considered a sign of disrespect. You could be severely reprimanded or worse if you try to challenge an instructor (not to mention pretty stupid too).

Humility, Mark of the Black Belt

I honestly feel that after you pass your black belt test, you can appreciate just about anything. Appreciation has a lot to do with humility. Humility is experienced when you realize how far you've come, but know how much farther you still have to go.

Once at a family gathering, we all piled into a car and I tried not to sit on the protruding seat belt clutch. My relatives made fun of me, asking, "Aren't you a black belt?" I laughed, but I also realized that now everyone, even my own family members, viewed me as a black belt along with all the super-hero capabilities that supposedly come with the rank.

That can create a lot of pressure. Just because you are a black belt doesn't mean you can part the Red Sea. There are still so many things to learn and to improve on. As a matter of fact, getting a black belt pretty much means that you are just learning how to walk in this ancient art.

Know the Do

Chodan, or first-degree black belt, literally means *the first step.* In Asia, first-degree black belts are a dime a dozen. You aren't considered to have been *down the road* until third- or fourth-degree or even higher.

Is a Black Belt Automatically a Qualified Teacher?

It is said that in Asia, students are more patient and more loyal than their American counterparts. In Korea, for example, students stay with their master for many years, perhaps even a lifetime. In this country, a student makes black belt and may soon decide he can move across town and set up his own school. But what often happens is that young black belt never advances in his own training. As time passes, he accumulates years but not knowledge. He teaches the same things in the same way over and over again. Although he claims to have 10 years of teaching experience, in reality he has only one year of teaching experience 10 times!

You've probably heard the statistic that only one in several hundred students who start out in the martial arts will ever make black belt. (In the old days when training was much more brutal the figures were more like one out of a thousand!) Even today, the student who makes black belt is a truly exceptional and dedicated individual. Discounting schools that hand out black belts after just a year or two, most organizations require four or five years of intense, demanding training. If you can make it through that, you are rare indeed.

Unfortunately no matter how good they are, some black belts never progress to learn the *higher* techniques. Many black belt instructors have also not been trained as teachers. They can do the techniques themselves but they can't show others how to do it. Good black belt instructors need to not only have superior instructional skills, but be able to communicate, demonstrate, and explain both technical and practical applications.

Martial Arts Minute

Some schools award a temporary or recommended black belt that the individual must wear for a predetermined amount of time to prove she is worthy of the permanent or decided black belt. Other schools just award the regular black belt right up front. Whichever your school does, it shouldn't be easy to attain.

But even going through these steps can't help an instructor with no communications skills. Even a beginning instructor who can get his ideas across is superior to a 10th-degree black belt who has no skills of communication. Good organizations make sure their instructors attend seminars, special classes, and do student-teaching under a experienced master instructor. In my own organization, instructors meet on a weekly basis to go over techniques and discuss business under the Grandmaster. No, not all black belts are qualified to teach. That is a skill that actually takes longer to develop than the ability to do kicking and punching.

So What Is a Black Belt?

Okay, let's look at some of the facts and figures about the fabled black belt. The dan rankings (or black belt levels) start at first-degree and go up to anywhere from sixth- to 10th-degree, depending on the martial arts system. In both the ITF and WTF Tae Kwon Do systems ninth is considered the highest because nine is the highest of the single-digit numbers. Other schools of Tae Kwon Do however, use the 10th-degree as the highest rank.

Usually promotions above fourth- or fifth-degree are based not on a physical test but on years of experience and the amount of contribution to the martial arts community. Contributions range from tournament wins to simply being a loyal and committed instructor.

Martial Arts Minute

In some schools, persons testing for second dan or higher have to do a specialty demonstration of some advanced area of martial arts study. This could be weapons, board breaking, self-defense, or even techniques from other systems. Usually a written thesis is also required for these higher ranks.

It usually takes 15 or more years as a black belt to attain master status. If someone tells you she is a master in Tae Kwon Do but has only been training for five or six years, someone is pulling your belt. In some Japanese and Okinawan systems, the belt changes color to red and black, red and white, or solid red at the Master levels. In some Korean systems however, the red belt is the rank below the black belt. And to add to the confusion, other Korean schools wear a black belt with a long red stripe running the entire length of the belt to signify a master level rank.

The minimum age for obtaining black belt also varies, but in most traditional schools it is 13 years or even more. There are *poom* belts or red and black belts given out in some schools for kids under the age of 13 to signify a junior black belt status. They will have to take the black belt test over again when they reach the required age.

In most systems a black belt must be senior by two ranks to promote another person. In other words, a second-degree black cannot test people for first *dan*. In the higher levels, this is sometimes reduced to one level because of the amount of time involved for promotion. The bottom line is, it takes a long time to get to the higher levels, and so there are relatively few people running around with seventh- or eighth-degree black belts (and none of them are in the sixth grade).

How Do You Earn a Black Belt?

The test for black belt is a big deal. It takes years of physical and mental preparation. I'll cover the specifics in Chapter 22, "Testing for the Big One," but for now just believe me that it is a life-changing experience. You'll look forward to it for years, and you'll look back on it for the rest of your life.

From Three to Eight Degrees of Separation

Know the Do
In some schools only black belts can wear an all black uniform. In many Tae Kwon Do schools, however, the only uniform anyone can wear is white, although the black belts can wear black trim around the lapel and bottom of the jacket. There are certain striping combinations allowed in other schools.

I have already stressed the importance of honoring and respecting any holder of a black belt. Address a black belt by either "Sa Bum" or his last name such as "Mr. Norris" or "Master Lee." The Korean names for the black belt ranks are:

1st degree Chodan

2nd degree Yidan

3rd degree Samdan

4th degree Sahdan

5th degree Ohdan

6th degree Yookdan

7th degree Childan

8th degree Paldan

9th degree Koodan

10th degree Sipdan

In many Tae Kwon Do schools, the black belts wear stripes on the end of their belts to signify their rank. Of course, if the person doesn't have stripes on his belt, you won't know his position. Better to just treat him like a 10th-degree and you won't be embarrassed later.

Master level black belts.

A Final Note on Black Belts

I can tell you personally that earning a black belt is a life-changing event. As a black belt, I now have compassion for white belts because I remember how hard it was when I first started my training. As a black belt, I never feel the need to use physical force for any reason. Although I know that I could, that is not the way a black belt resolves conflict. If my black belt were ever stolen or destroyed, still no one could ever take it away from me because I always wear it in my heart.

Finally, as a black belt, I am more humbled now than ever, realizing how much a student of life I really am.

The Least You Need to Know

➤ Black belts come in all shapes and sizes, but all their hearts are big.

➤ It should take several years to earn a black belt.

➤ Not all black belts are qualified to teach. Just because someone is a teacher for 10 years doesn't mean they have 10 years of teaching experience.

➤ A black belt test is purposefully hard so you will appreciate and value your accomplishment.

➤ Master and Grandmaster ranks are very rare because not many individuals can stay dedicated to one activity for an entire lifetime.

Stupid
written
exam...

Chapter 21

Testing...One, Two, Three

In This Chapter

➤ Knowing when you take a test

➤ Understanding what's involved in taking tests

➤ Knowing what to do if you mess up

➤ Waiting to get your belt

You have dreaded tests since the first grade. Math, science, English composition, yikes! Then there were your driving tests, blood tests, maybe even typing or fitness tests. Some you did okay on, others, well, let's just say that testing was never your forte.

Some people test well, that is, they can study and go into a testing situation confident and relaxed and do their best. Other people freeze up no matter how much they may have prepared.

Martial arts tests can be more stressful than you can imagine. Not only is there the fear of looking like an idiot, but if you mess up, you can get punched or kicked around. The physical factor adds a whole other dimension to the testing scenario.

Testing is a part of Tae Kwon Do that you can't avoid if you want to climb up that rank ladder to black belt. And if you know what to expect, it can be a very exciting part of your training.

Why Can't They Just Give Me the Darn Belt?

Some people think that if the instructor thinks you are a green-belt-level student, then he ought to just award you the belt and let it go at that. Well, in some schools that's exactly what they do. You never ask to test. You never know when or where the test is. The instructor might not even let you know that he is evaluating you for the belt that moment. He just says to you one night that you are now an orange belt or blue belt or whatever.

That may seem like a good way to do it, but there are advantages to putting someone through a specific and often intensive testing situation. For one, it reveals how you react under pressure. If you screw up and forget practically everything you are supposed to know, then how do you expect to perform in a real life-and-death situation? If you can't remember what to do or if you can't make yourself do it right, then you might as well not have learned it at all.

Belt testing is a good indication of your mind, your heart, and your body. That's why almost every martial arts school has regular testing for the students.

Hey Kids, What Time Is It?

When do you test? When you are ready of course, but let's get more specific here. Most schools have a consistent testing schedule. It might be on the last Thursday of the month or every first Saturday of the quarter.

But don't try to take the test unless you know your stuff. Many students, especially the kids, want to take the test as soon as they are eligible time-wise. Just because you have been a yellow belt for four months (or whatever period your school deems necessary) doesn't mean you can take that next test. You have to know the required techniques, and, beyond that, you have to be able to perform them in front of the judges.

Wise Sa Bum Tells Us

Your instructor will be able to determine when you are ready to test. Even if you don't feel ready at the time, trust his instincts. He's not out to steer you the wrong way.

Free or Fee?

For years martial arts schools have charged a fee for belt promotions. Some schools today include the cost of the test in the regular tuition at the school, so you don't have to pay any extra on test day. We don't have any objections to a testing fee as long as it reasonable and includes the cost of your belt, certificates, handouts, certain boards, and the like.

(If your instructor teaches through a community recreation center or YMCA, then he has to buy the test sheets, the boards, the belts, the certificates, and anything else himself. So a fee for an exam is certainly reasonable.)

What's the Basic Set-Up?

Only black belts and higher are allowed to grade student tests. Usually there is a table set up at the front of the Do Jang where the judges sit to watch you and possibly write down mistakes you may make on examination sheets.

In most schools the judges will be dressed in their fanciest uniforms or in a coat and tie. Test days are important occasions, and everyone should look and act the part.

Students will sit quietly at the back of the school waiting for their name to be called. Be sure to yell out, "Yes sir," or "Yes ma'am" when you hear your name. Run to the proper area and snap into a nice ready position. The judges will tell you what to do next.

When your part of the test is done, be sure to walk backward out of the area to your seat. Always sit erect, with your legs folded in the correct position, and be quiet so you won't disturb the other students testing. You want the same courtesy from them when you are up there.

> **Martial Arts Minute**
> In some federations or associations you have to pay a fee to the *home office* for rank certification. Reasonable fees are a few dollars (U.S.) for lower ranks to upwards of $100 for a fancy, oversized, framed, translated from Korean or Japanese, black belt certificate.

> **Know the Do**
> You will not only have to obey commands in Korean but you might even have to say a few. A common command you'll say a lot at a test is charyot-kyung yay, or *attention bow*.

A test board consists of all black belts.

The Order of the Day

Since the lower ranks usually go first, white belts testing for yellow will be the first group up. So if there are a lot of people testing on this particular day, you may have to wait a while. Remember to sit still and watch quietly. Many times your discipline while you wait is also considered part of your test.

Some schools allow the tests to be conducted in groups so intermediate students don't have to sit and wait through all the beginners.

Often the advanced or black belts test on a separate day altogether. This makes these test even more special and gives the rest of the students of the school the opportunity to come and watch the *big guys* test.

Who Does the Grading?

In some schools you have to be a third-degree black belt to even sit on the test board, but in other schools any black belt has earned the privilege of being a judge. And it is a privilege. What happens on this day often determines whether or not a student stays or possibly quits his or her martial arts training.

It varies from school to school, but rarely can a junior black belt actually grade students and pass them to the next rank. In some cases, a junior black belt can add comments on the test sheet but he cannot do any actual promotions. All promotions are, of course, under the direction of the master instructor.

A, B, C

Normally there are not grades such as A or B, or even number grades like 98 or 75. Some schools do assign a certain number of points to each section of a test, but usually it's kind of a pass/fail situation. After watching all the requirements and writing down comments the judge simply asks himself, "Does this student deserve a green belt or not?"

There is still some leeway for the judge to make a determination, for example, pass-plus, pass, pass-minus, and no-pass. But usually it is a judgment call.

Wise Sa Bum Tells Us

It may seem unfair, but often you are judged based on your comparison to the other students taking the test that day. If you look better than them, you'll probably pass. If you stink compared to the others, then you may fail.

If you mess up on one part of the test, that doesn't mean you automatically fail. Everything is taken into consideration. If you forget something, like a move of a form, just go back to ready position and ask permission to start over again. Of course some parts of the test are more important than others. Forgetting one move of a form is not as critical as getting the crap beat out of you by everyone else on the test, including that four-year-old and the great, great grandmother.

Just How Hard Is It?

Even after all the above warnings about paying attention and being sure not to screw up, remember that most instructors take the position that martial arts should be a confidence-building experience. What that means is, they don't want to see you fail, and they hate not passing a student onto a higher rank.

Of course there are pretty tough standards for the higher, more advanced ranks but at the lower *gup* levels the judges are pretty lenient. They know that you are very, very nervous. So usually, if you mess up, they just chalk that up to nervousness, and you're not going to fail.

One of the key elements here is how hard you try. If you are screaming your heart out and shouting "Yes sir" every chance you get, the judges will no doubt be impressed by your attitude. Remember that this is not only a physical test but a test of your spirit. When you are nervous, you probably tend to clam up, but you must force yourself to do the opposite. If you go through the test with this kind of spirit-filled attitude, we can almost guarantee that you will not fail, no matter how badly you might feel you did.

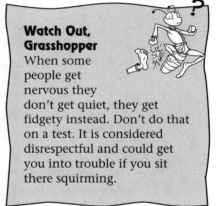

Know the Do
Gup, meaning *grade*, ranks are the ranks below black belt. *Dan* or *degree* signifies the black belt ranks.

Watch Out, Grasshopper
When some people get nervous they don't get quiet, they get fidgety instead. Don't do that on a test. It is considered disrespectful and could get you into trouble if you sit there squirming.

TAE KWON DO
YELLOW BELT EXAM

Date
$10 Fee Paid ☐
(This fee is to reimburse your instructor for the cost of the belt, certificate and class handouts.)

Name _____ Age _____

How long in Tae Kwon Do? _____ Instructor(s) _____

Signature (of parent/guardian if under 18) _____
   By signing this form I acknowledge that my child has my permission to participate in this martial arts examination.

ANSWER THIS QUESTION:
How do we build self-confidence? _____

_____

FILL OUT THE ABOVE, ATTACH $10 AND BRING YOU TO THE TEST. **NOTE:** The fee reimburses your teacher for the certificate, belt and handouts. (You can take a makeup test with no extra fee if you do not pass the first time.) <u>MAKE CHECKS OUT TO A-KATO.</u>

BLOCKING
9-step Block

PUNCHING
Horse Stance / punching

KICKING
Front Snap Kick
Side Snap Kick

SELF-DEFENSE
Front choke
Wrist grab
Hair grab

☐ Excellent (Plus+)   ☐ Good   ☐ Passible but some improvement needed (Minus –)   ☐ No promotion

E = EXCELLENT	G = GOOD	I = IMPROVEMENT NEEDED	
ATTITUDE IN CLASS (DISCIPLINE)	EFFORT		RESPECT

Examiner _____   Promoted to _____

© 1996, American Karate And Tae Kwon Do Organization

Test form example 1.

Young Brothers TAE KWON-DO
Application for Color Belt Test

THIS SPACE FOR STUDENT

Date of Test: _____
Mo. / Day / Yr.

Name: _____ Sex: Male ____ Female ____
Last   First   M. Init.

Address: _____
Street   City   State   Zip

Date of Birth: _____ Age: _____ Occupation: _____
Mo. / Day / Yr.

Phone # : _____ Height: _____ Weight: _____ Belt Size: ____

Current Belt Level: _____ Belt Grade # : _____

I desire to be examined for a higher belt and grade in the Art of TAE KWON-DO.

Student: _____ Parent (If under 18): _____
Signature   Signature

DO NOT WRITE BELOW - OFFICIAL SPACE FOR EXAMINER
Examiner's Scoring System

99 Maximum
85 Lowest Passing Level   Score

	Score
Ki Hap - Breath Control - Eye Contact	
Power - Speed - Balance	
Concentration & Correctness of Technique	
Combinations	
SA - JU - JI - RU - KI	
CHON - JI	
DAN - GUN	
DO - SAN	
WON - HYO	
YUL - GOK	
JOONG - GUN	
TOI - GYE	
HWA - RANG	
CHOONG - MOO	
One Steps	
Free Sparing	
Breaking	
Terminology	
Student's Total Score	
Student's Average Score	

Pass _____ Fail _____ Examiner's Signature _____

Test form example 2.

Clean Up First

At this point we shouldn't even have to tell you to wash and press your uniform before showing up to test, but you would be amazed at how many kids come to a belt promotion with grass stains on their knees. Your hair should be combed, your face washed, your nails clipped, your jewelry left at home. Come to the Do Jang as though you are coming to an important event. It is.

Watch Me!

If you have little kids, you know they are always wanting someone to watch them do something, especially something that they have accomplished. This is your chance, parents, to watch your kids really accomplish something impressive. Feel free to bring your cameras or bring the grandparents. Everyone should be able to share in this experience.

And believe it or not, even teenagers and adults need the kind of encouragement that comes from showing off in front of someone you are close to and receiving their admiration. That means that you should come to watch your 15-year-old get his blue belt and that you should encourage your wife in her proud accomplishment when she earns that first yellow belt.

Wise Sa Bum Tells Us

If your loved one fails to earn that belt, for whatever reason, do not say something like, "Well, you messed that up didn't you?" Give him encouragement and say how proud you are that he even tried. Taking a Tae Kwon Do test takes guts.

Give 'em a Break

Since Tae Kwon Do is a style known for breaking techniques, many schools begin board-breaking right at the very beginning. Sometimes you have to break a single, inch-thick, white pine board to advance to the yellow belt level. Others schools wait several months until you build up enough confidence and skills.

Board-breaking isn't nearly as tough as you might think; however, it does take some instruction and some getting used to (so don't try this at home). Usually you will not have to break more than two or three boards together, and even that is at the advanced stages. You probably will see several *station* breaks where students must break a board in two or three directions, all without stopping. Breaking the wood isn't the hardest part, it's spinning or turning in all directions while maintaining balance and power. Initially, it will probably be only a single board. The breaks get harder as you climb in rank.

On a final note, you may have seen guys on TV and in tournament demonstrations break big stacks of boards or even blocks of ice, but remember that those are highly trained individuals who have practiced long and hard for those kinds of feats.

Test Etiquette

We have already mentioned much of the proper etiquette in other chapters, but on test day all these rules go double! Bow to every black belt you see. Ask permission before you do anything. No talking. By now you have been in class for a while, and you should know the drill.

By the way, resist the urge to giggle or laugh at someone when they mess up, even if it's funny. And don't laugh if you mess up, even if it's because you are nervous. By the same token, don't cry if you can't do something, like break your board, just keep trying until you can. You're almost always given another chance. Remember that attitude is often more important than your physical skill at the early stages.

> **Martial Arts Minute**
> In the early days of martial arts practice in America, some masters broke boards and bricks to get the Americans' attention. Today everyone seems to think board-breaking is a bigger part of the martial arts than it really is. Board-breaking is a test of your aim and power and ability to "see through" challenging situations.

> **Watch Out, Grasshopper**
> Mom and Dad, make sure little Johnny (or Susie) goes to the bathroom *before* the test so he won't go *during* the test.

When Do You Get Belted?

Most schools award the colored belts and accompanying certificates right after the test. Some Do Jangs make you wait until the next class until you are given the belt to wear. Other schools actually make you wait through a probationary period to see if you really deserve your new rank. The only exception is becoming a black belt, which may take months.

Whenever it might be, you should feel proud of your accomplishment because few people have either the confidence or the skill to get out there in front of the judges and take that test. Tae Kwon Do promotional exams are a very important part of your journey to black belt.

The Least You Need to Know

➤ Martial arts tests are stressful for a reason—to build your confidence.

➤ Don't ask to test, but wait until your instructor says you are ready and then practice hard.

➤ At the lower stages, attitude can be the most important part of the exam.

➤ If you mess up, just relax and ask to start again.

Testing for the Big One

Everyone has the potential of becoming a black belt. Almost everyone who starts martial arts wants to be a black belt someday. Unfortunately, the statistics show that most people who sign up for Tae Kwon Do lessons will quit before earning their black belt. The fact remains that few people achieve their potential. You can be one of the few who do, however, if you apply yourself.

Why do most Tae Kwon Do students not last until black belt? Reasons for this vary from not enough time to train to not enough money to continue lessons to losing interest altogether. These are all valid reasons, but only you can determine how important it is to you to keep training in the martial arts until you get to the magical point where you are ready to take that big test for the black belt. Don't get discouraged; even if you don't feel like you'll ever be ready, there are ways you can achieve this goal.

I know I am repeating myself, but earning a black belt can and will change your life. You will mark the day of your birth, the day you graduated from high school, got married, had your first child, and the day you made black belt as among the most important days of your life.

Time Is of the Essence

You already know that different schools have different minimum time requirements for black belt. But I'm not talking about the chronological time in months or years here; I mean the right time in your head and heart. Your instructor is the best judge of that. Often beginning students want to test before they are actually ready. I am always listening to some little boy or girl begging to be allowed to test for orange or green belt way before they are ready.

However, it is very rare for someone to ask to test for black belt early. Not only is that unacceptable by martial arts standards (you never tell your instructor when you are going to do something in your training—he tells you), it also runs contrary to the very spirit of a dedicated student. The student trains to perfect himself or herself rather than to achieve glory.

Trust me though, your instructor is also looking forward to you becoming a black belt. There is nothing quite like the pride of having a student of yours achieve this level in his or her career. Your teachers care about you, and becoming one of their black belts, in essence, makes you one of their family.

Your instructor, therefore, will carefully watch you and guide you to this all-important point. If you are an advanced student, close to black belt, in every class the teacher is silently evaluating you, gauging your readiness. While you may wonder if you are able to pass that test, the master instructor probably has already made up his or her mind about you. He will tell you when you are ready to test.

The black belt test is actually much more than just a physical examination. It is an examination of a person's character and ability to serve as a role model for the other students in the school. If you are told that you can test for the black belt, it is a sure bet that the master thinks you are ready for all the responsibilities that come with the rank.

In my own school, a student is a chodan candidate for at least 12 months before the actual test. During this time, the instructor gives periodic "pre-tests," checking the various requirements and techniques for first-degree black belt. Of course, these include the mental, emotional, physical, and character aspects he deems necessary.

Martial Arts Minute

In the early days of the martial arts in this country (the '50s and '60s), black belt tests were, for lack of a better word, brutal. The arts were just being established in America, and the practitioners wanted everyone to know how effective they really were. It was not uncommon to see broken bones and teeth (and candidates) knocked out.

Know the Do

Chodan is a first-degree black belt. Literally the word means *first step*, indicating that you have taken the first step toward mastering the art.

Once You Have Been Given the Stamp of Approval

After your instructor gives you permission to test, the real preparation begins. It might be weeks or months before the actual day of the exam, but you must start to prepare both physically and mentally. Training with other people is valuable. You'll need to spend time on your own to mentally prepare as well. Many find that just hitting the heavy bag alone or repeating your forms in the back yard is one of the best ways to begin to steel your mind for the task at hand.

If you haven't already set up a proper diet, this is the time to do so. Don't skip breakfast. Don't eat late at night. Go light on coffee and other forms of caffeine. You have already quit smoking haven't you? Stay away from unnecessary fat, salt, sugar, and other things that aren't on the list of good diets. Be sure and eat plenty of fruits and vegetables. (If you are lucky, you might even form good eating habits that will stick with you for the rest of your life.)

Start to train in some aspect on a daily basis. That might mean getting up early to do some stretching and sit ups or push-ups in your bedroom before your morning shower. It might mean going out for a run after you come home from school or work. Certainly it means going to the Do Jang every chance you get.

Since the test will involve demonstrating all your techniques, you must remember them—practically in your sleep. That translates into constant drilling of your kicks, forms, and one-steps. If you have a martial arts partner to work out with, all the better. If there is more than one of you testing on the same day, and many schools set it up that way, train with your testing partners—a lot!

Finally, take the last couple of days off to rest. Believe me, you won't learn anything new in 48 hours, if you don't already know by now. You'll need the time to just relax and to prepare yourself mentally.

> **Know the Do**
> Many schools conduct the tests entirely in Korean. Even if yours doesn't, there will be plenty of Korean terminology thrown at you. Nothing is more embarrassing than forgetting the commands during your black belt test. So be sure to study.

The Day Itself

No matter what time of day the test is scheduled for, get up early to meditate and to prepare yourself mentally for the challenge. Eat a hearty breakfast. Athletes eat lots of carbohydrates (called carbohydrate-packing) on the day of a big game. Pancakes are good for this. Don't eat too much either. I have seen some people get so nervous or so tired that they actually throw up during the test.

However, if you are like me, you get too nervous to eat at all. But make yourself eat something! Even a few crackers and some tea will get your blood sugar up enough to get you through this grueling day.

Get to the school early so you won't feel rushed when you arrive. Give yourself time to change into your uniform and to stretch. Have all your equipment set and ready to go. Bring a water bottle or a nutrient thirst quencher. A towel is a good idea also.

Lastly, relax. Sure this is a big day, but it's a big day that you'll want to have fun experiencing. It is often said that football players or other athletes that just go out and have a good time end up playing much better than if they are too uptight. Of course that is easier said than done, but if your martial arts training has taught you anything, it should be to relax and perform well under pressure.

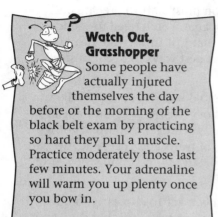

Watch Out, Grasshopper
Some people have actually injured themselves the day before or the morning of the black belt exam by practicing so hard they pull a muscle. Practice moderately those last few minutes. Your adrenaline will warm you up plenty once you bow in.

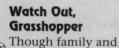

Watch Out, Grasshopper
Though family and friends will want to spectate this big event, asking them not to is understandable. There will be plenty of time for fanfare the day black belts are awarded.

Here Comes the Judge

Who will sit on the panel of judges that will determine your fate? Your own master instructor, of course, and probably the other black belts in your school (however, someone must be two ranks above you to be able to vote). There may also be visiting masters and guests from other schools in your federation. All in all, it will probably be a pretty intimidating lineup.

It depends on the school as to who will conduct the test itself. Sometimes the master will just sit there, silently observing, while the second in command barks out all the orders. In other schools, the master will conduct the exam, usually throwing in some surprises. Sometimes he makes the candidates run laps around the block before the test. I have seen some candidates have to do 10 push-ups between each form (after a dozen forms that equals 120 push-ups).

What's Actually Involved?

Believe it or not, what is involved is actually a controversial subject. Some schools put tremendous emphasis on the physical performance on the mat. The slightest mess-up can flunk you. The test is long and arduous.

Other instructors have already made up their minds about you in the previous weeks so that the actual test day is only a confirmation of what they have already decided. The test is demanding, to be sure, but it isn't the make-or-break factor in deciding if you will become a black belt.

Because I don't know which way your particular school leans, I can only tell you about my own experiences and requirements. We were taught that this is the biggest day of your martial arts life, and, as such, needs to be a day you will remember. That means the black belt test is the culmination of years of physical and mental preparation.

It signifies that you will be qualified, after this test, to teach the basics of the art to beginners because you yourself have mastered these basic techniques. Therefore the black belt exam should involve a demonstration of all the basic requirements for every belt level up to and including the black belt. This alone could take an hour or more. Some masters have the candidate actually teach a basic technique or two to demonstrate her abilities in this area.

The Fight of Your Life

Some schools require just a few sparring matches to show the examining board that you have the technique required for the black belt rank. Other associations or federations demand a dozen matches or more. Often this includes fighting multiple opponents—two, three, or four persons at once. Normally you will have to fight other black belts.

Keep in mind that the other black belts have more experience than you (and they probably aren't as tired as you will be by the time you actually get around to sparring them). You aren't supposed to allow them to beat you up unmercifully either. If you want to join the ranks, you have to be able to hold your own against other black belts. That means keeping your hands up even though you may be dead tired. It means hanging in there and not giving up even if the other person is much bigger than you are.

Attitude plays a bigger role than you might think. No matter what happens, whatever they may ask you to do, show that indomitable spirit.

The master may intentionally put you up against someone you probably could never beat in a real fight (maybe a great big, fourth-degree black belt, for example). He doesn't want to see you get beat up, even though it may seem that way; he wants to see your inner spirit and strength come out under pressure. The point is to take the candidate to the point of pure physical exhaustion and then see if he can still perform at an acceptable level. I have seen some people pass out right in the middle of the test, and many a person has given up and had to take the grueling test all over again.

Martial Arts Minute
What kind of score do you have to make to pass a black belt? Some masters require the equivalent of an "A." Perfection is practically demanded. Some require a unanimous vote on the part of all the eligible judges. Even one dissenter could force you to take the test over again. Other candidates only need the consent of the head instructor. The bottom line is, do so well that everyone present will give you that "A."

Usually the fighting comes toward the end of the test after a demonstration of all the forms, kicks, self-defense, and one-steps. I have heard it said that these things are the elements of the test that you can control—in others words it is up to you whether or not you do your kicks and forms correctly. The fighting, on the other hand, is out of your control. You can't choose your opponents for this day.

Give Me a Break!

Usually there are stacks of boards or concrete blocks to break on a black belt test. My school requires a three-station break—that is, board breaks with three different techniques in three different directions all done without stopping. Some schools require concrete breaks and/or jumping kick board breaks.

You'll probably have practiced these breaks many times before the actual test. There are even plastic, re-breakable boards you can buy that will enable you to break a board hundreds of times without having to set up a revolving charge account at the lumber yard. In any case, approach the break on the test with a positive attitude. Meditate silently before attempting the break, and don't forget to yell loudly.

Watch Out, Grasshopper

Breaking techniques seem to be a bigger part of the Korean martial arts than in some other styles for some reason. Although breaking is certainly impressive, it can also be dangerous. In fact, some surveys have shown breaking to be the one area of martial arts training that causes more injuries than sparring. So always learn proper technique from your instructor, and don't try any fancy breaks on your own until you are really experienced.

Know the Do

The actual martial art of weapons is called Kobudo, or *old warrior ways*. It is an Okinawan system, although many other arts, including Tae Kwon Do make use of the Kobudo weapons.

Pick Your Weapons

Oftentimes the candidate will have to know and show how to defend against knives and clubs. The main idea on weapons defense is not to get sliced or clonked while you are blocking. Control of the weapon is primary as you move out of the way and counterstrike. This can be one of the most impressive parts of the test for the spectators (and humorous).

Some Do Jangs will also require the black belt candidate to know how to use weapons. This can be the simple club or knife, or it could be the use of the popular martial arts weapons like the *nunchaku* or *bo* staff. Some systems of Tae Kwon Do even have required forms with certain weapons.

The Write Stuff

Lastly, there are written requirements for the black belt. At our school we have to turn in an essay and take a verbal test on exam day. Questions are on topics like history and etiquette.

Below is a sample written test for a first-degree black belt. Can you answer these questions?

BLACK BELT WRITTEN TEST
All questions taken from the A-KaTo Instructor's Manual

1. What were the *Kwans* in post World War II Korea?

2. When did the name *Tae Kwon Do* come into official usage?

3. Tae Kwon Do was chosen in part because the word is similar to an ancient Korean martial art. Which one?

4. Which came first, the *International* TKD Fed., or the *World* TKD Fed.?

5. . Who formed the first *Karate* school in Japan?

6. When, and what was it called?

7. Who introduced TKD to America and when?

8. What does the Yin/Yang (Um/Yang) symbolize?

10. What are the *Tenets of Tae Kwon Do*?

11. Name three deseased martial artists and their contributions.

12. What are five characteristics of a black belt instructor.

13. Name three martial arts books that you own and give a one paragraph description of each.

ESSAY QUESTION
What is the difference between an internal and an external martial art?

Sample black belt written exam form.

What If You Flunk?

I know you don't even want to think about this, but it might happen. People flunk for whatever reasons. Maybe they just blank-out and forget what they are supposed to do. Perhaps they are out-of-shape and run out of steam. Whatever the case, they will have to do it all over again at another time and place. Some schools require a candidate who has failed a test wait up to six months before she can test again. Others allow a re-test in just another month or so. Actually, if you don't pass a black belt exam, it will probably take you a couple of months just to get over the emotional drain of the experience.

Some people, of course, never come back after failing a black belt test. Of course, you might say then they were never worth a black belt in the first place, but as I said in the first few paragraphs of this chapter, everyone has the potential to make black belt. If you didn't the first time, you just have to pick yourself up and try again. You have no doubt heard the saying, "Quitters aren't those who fall down, quitters are those who don't get back up again after they fall."

What If You Pass?

Congratulations, you've sweated, toiled, waited, and you've finally passed! Nothing can compare to that feeling. Take plenty of photos (you'll treasure them in years to come). Thank your training partners and your instructor, for without all of them, you would never have made it to this point.

Now, of course, you can take those next steps on your way to becoming a master yourself. As far away as that may seem, you need to have your next goal in mind. You have just begun the journey of a lifetime of the study of the martial arts. You are one of the fraternity, the brotherhood of black belts. It carries with it a great responsibility because you are now an example to all those who would follow you and would be like you...a black belt!

> **Martial Arts Minute**
> Black belt ceremonies where the actual belt and/or certificate are awarded are very formal occasions. Some schools hold these right away at the conclusion of the examination. Others wait days or even weeks. Some masters actually tie the belts on the new black belt's waists. Others present them in a kneeling and bowed position. Whatever your school does, it represents a great moment for you.

But don't go getting a big head! At my black belt ceremony, our Grandmaster awarded our belts and certificates and then concluded our momentous day with this statement, "Congratulations, you now know how to walk." Believe me, there's a whole new ballgame headed your way.

Upon receiving your black belt, you don't just all of a sudden become enlightened with the knowledge of a ninja. You have to grow into your belt, and you will soon discover that you are going to feel like a white belt all over again. That feeling of being a dork, a big, clumsy ox seems to find its way back to you right when you think you've learned everything there is to know. That's why you become more humble the higher you climb in rank; you finally start to realize how little you really do know. Not just about Tae Kwon Do, but about life in general.

Being a Black Belt Everywhere

Then there's having to deal with the peer pressure of being expected to be Bruce Lee all of the time, but with better control. And never doubt this for one minute, you are being watched at all times. Not just by all of the junior belts in class, but by your co-workers, your classmates, the entire community! Welcome to the world of not being able to mess up. For example, if you go out and get sloshed at your local tavern, you bring shame to your school, your instructor, and your art, not to mention all the other students who will follow your every lead and go out and get sloshed too. You are, in essence, becoming a Michael Jordan–type hero to all the people you come in contact with. If you can't handle this kind of pressure, then don't even think about becoming a black belt. That piece of black material carries with it more meaning than most people will ever realize.

The Least You Need to Know

➤ Your instructor will let you know when you are ready to take the black belt test.

➤ Preparation for that single day should take weeks or even months.

➤ Your master will be joined by other judges who will all have to recognize your abilities.

➤ Your actual test will consist of a demonstration of all your techniques and will probably include board breaking, weapons, a written or verbal test, and lots of sparring.

➤ Remember, the first-degree black belt is considered only the first step of your training. Now you are ready to start learning the deeper aspects of the art.

Part 6
The Wide, Wide World of Competition

Competition is perhaps the most controversial element of modern Tae Kwon Do. Some people love it, while others wish it would go away. But being an Olympic sport, Tae Kwon Do competition is here to stay. There are differences in the many avenues of sporting martial arts.

Moving up the ladder from white belt to black belt and everything in between is one of the best ways to test your abilities and to gain a supreme sense of self-accomplishment. Learn why and how to travel the colored-belt road.

Chapter 23

Be a Sport: An Intro to the World of Competition

In This Chapter

➤ Learning how tournaments got started

➤ Comparing open tournaments with closed competitions

➤ Understanding when you will be ready to compete

➤ Knowing what to do when you lose big time

➤ Finding that lessons can be learned from both losing and winning

Martial arts competitions are not, as some would have you believe, ancient practices. In the old days, and we mean hundreds or thousands of years ago, the Asian warriors never thought of fighting just for fun. The warrior ways were for life-and-death struggles, not for awards to hang or place in your home.

Yet, we do not live in ancient times where tribes and nations are constantly at war. There is no battlefield to test our skills. (Sure there are the mean streets of your particular town or city but no sane person would intentionally get into a fight just for fun.)

Tournaments, modern sport competitions, are one of the best ways to face the challenges of an unknown opponent while staying safe at the same time. And they can be fun too.

Martial Arts Minute

In 1964, Tae Kwon Do stylist J. Pat Burleson won Jhoon Rhee's first U.S. National Karate Championships in Washington D.C. and became the first star of American martial arts competition. Burleson went on to win several more championships earning the nickname, "the grandaddy of American sport Karate."

A Modern Thing

As we've said, tournaments are fairly modern inventions. In fact Judo is thought to have been the first martial art to stage competitions in the late 19th century. Japanese Karate began to have matches in the early 20th century (something that really ticked off the Okinawan traditionalists who said competition was the death knell of the art).

Americans, however, took Karate tournaments to new heights soon after the martial arts were introduced in the United States. In 1960 they began to have small competitions in various parts of the country, and by 1963 the Americans had begun to hold the first truly national championships with competitors coming from several states.

Who Can Enter?

Anybody can compete in local tournaments provided your school approves of the event. Your instructor will normally tell you about tournaments you can compete in. And more than likely, your school has probably participated in most of these tournaments for years.

Sometimes you'll run into a tournament poster in a storefront window, or you may even get an invitation to compete at a tournament in the mail. Why should you always get permission first? First of all, it's considered disrespectful not to. Your teacher may know who's running the tournament and may feel it is unsafe for you to compete. He may also not be aware of who's running it, and you could find yourself caught up in a really tough situation with different rules and regulations, which could also put your safety into jeopardy.

When Are Tournaments Held?

In the northern states, tournaments are held either in the spring or fall to avoid inclement weather for those traveling out of town. In California they hold tournaments every weekend. Most of your local tournaments will be open to all ranks, white belt to black, and literally all ages.

Wise Sa Bum Tells Us

Parents, be ready to spend all day at a tournament. Some moms and dads think they will just drop their kids off and pick them up in a couple hours. Don't plan on it. Besides, it is a great way to spend some quality time with your kid.

Where Are Competitions Held?

Tournaments can be held in anything from a high school gym to a hotel ballroom. If you do have permission to compete, check into pre-registering. Usually if you do so, you'll get a discount in competition fees. Keep in mind that competing can get expensive, especially if you're traveling out of town. Unless your school has sold donuts or magazines for the past year, you'll have to come up with the funds yourself.

The Worldly Games

Today everyone seems to have a big name for their tournament, "The World Championships," or "The Intergalactic Games." The truth is, there is no ultimate martial arts championships (not even those on pay-per-view). It's hard enough to get people together at an open tournament let alone the closed events. So no, you will never know who the toughest guy or girl really is because there is always someone out there who won't or can't compete in a particular event no matter how cool-sounding the name may be.

Open or Closed?

Open tournaments are just that, they are *open* to anyone who wants to enter them. So Karate, Tae Kwon Do, and even Kung Fu stylists can be seen at a typical open event. Obviously there is a lot of variety, and for that reason they can be fun to watch and challenging to compete in. But there are drawbacks too. Sometimes the fighters from different styles don't understand all the rules, and that makes for hard feelings and sometimes conflict between competitors and judges. It shouldn't be that way, but it lots of times is.

Closed tournaments, on the other hand, are held just for the students of a particular school or association. The Olympic Tae Kwon Do style tournaments of the WTF are, in essence, closed competitions because you have to be a member of their sanctioned bodies. Although that doesn't sit well with the millions of Tae Kwon Do practitioners in the world that don't belong to such groups, it does make for consistent and usually well-run tournaments. Plus there is the possibility of earning a spot on the Olympic team.

Full-Contact

Let's say just a word about full-contact tournaments here. Most competitions are what is called no-contact or semi-contact. That means the idea is not to knock out the opponent but to win by scoring points. But in full-contact competition, often just called *kick boxing*, the best way to win is to kick or punch your opponent's lights out. These matches are reserved for the serious professional fighter and are not to be tried by the just-curious.

Point tournaments are usually pretty safe. There are rules about protective equipment and rules about where you can and can't hit. You'll also more than likely be fighting those of your same rank and size or age. Don't worry about being in one of those death matches from a Jean Claude Van Damme movie—that's strictly Hollywood.

Tournaments May Not be Your Bag

Some students never try their hand (or foot) at competing at tournaments. The truth is, it can be very scary and it's always a lot of hard work. And though accidents can happen, there's always a chance you can get hurt. Some older students, for example, just don't want to get out there and fight with the younger guys (although there are divisions for more mature competitors).

Some of the more traditionalist schools do not promote or even allow tournaments altogether. They feel that the whole idea of learning the martial arts so that you can go out and win trophies or medals is not what should be on your mind when you sign up for Karate.

However, having said all that, tournaments properly done can be a great way to advance your skills and teach some valuable lessons about things like hard work, sportsmanship, and the ability to gracefully accept either victory or defeat.

The Agony of Defeat

Early in my career I competed in a tournament and felt sure that I was gypped because I had landed a lot of scoring punches, but the judges just wouldn't call them. Anxious and eager to come home with my first trophy, I went up to my Grandmaster at the head table and told him that I thought the fighting competition was unfair. He very calmly grabbed a trophy off of the table and handed it to me saying "Here, you take this." As I bowed and took the trophy that I didn't earn, my heart sank. That plastic and marble statue meant absolutely nothing to me, and I gave it back before the tournament was over. Here I learned my first lesson about winning. It didn't seem so important after that.

Watch Out, Grasshopper

In a big city there are probably martial arts tournaments every few weeks. Before you go check one out, though, ask your instructor about it. Some schools don't want you going to tournaments except ones that their own organization sanctions.

Going for the Gold

Okay, so winning isn't everything, but it feels really great to get a medal or trophy. So what's the big prize for your effort? Sometimes you're awarded medals that are worth less than the entry fee of the tournament. But in some of the big events you can get trophies that are as tall as you are. Generally speaking, the bigger the prizes, the more people will be there to try and win them.

Some events even have prize money for the black belt divisions. The amount varies, but often it is called expense money and comes to a couple hundred dollars or so.

When Are You Ready to Step in the Ring?

Many a student has signed up for a tournament and at the last minute decided not to compete because he or she didn't feel ready.

But you should know that even the most serious competitors won't ever tell you that they feel *ready*. There are times when you might feel lucky, but never truly ready. Basically, you just have to get out there and try it, ready or not. I highly encourage all students to try competing at least once in their martial arts career. Yes, it can be very trying, but it will prove to be very rewarding if you win, and even more rewarding if you lose!

Know the Do
Better learn the terminology before you go to a tournament. The Korean word for *stop* for example is *go-mahn*, which can sound a lot like "go man."

Fear of Losing

A concerned parent once told me that she did not want her little boy to compete because he might lose, and that would hurt his feelings. I said "Yes it will hurt his feelings, and that's why you should let him compete."

We feel that children need to know what it's like to lose, because, the fact is, they are not going to win at everything in life. Even as adults, there is something about losing that makes you grow on the inside. I've learned a lot from the times that I have been fortunate enough to win, but I have learned even more from the times that I have lost. Not just on how to improve my fighting or perfect my forms, but how to really appreciate things.

You see, the one who wins first place most of the time often feels disappointed at coming in second or third. But the student who never wins literally jumps for joy if he places even third or fourth. Losing can truly teach you an appreciation for winning.

Losing also makes you appreciate hard work and dedication because you keep trying harder to get better. Sometimes those who are *natural athletes* and win every division they compete in are very shallow because they have no appreciation for their God-given ability. But when you see a housewife win, who hasn't been physical since high school, you can feel her appreciation for all the hard work she's put into competing.

The bottom line is look forward to both winning and losing when you compete. If you win, congratulate yourself. And if you lose, also congratulate yourself because you have learned a valuable lesson about yourself and life.

Wise Sa Bum Tells Us

Loosing in a martial arts match has no bearing on your status in life. In fact some of the most consistent losers in tournaments are the biggest successes in other areas because they have learned the lessons of defeat.

The Confidence Factor

So, it is not a matter of winning or losing you should concentrate on but rather having the confidence to just get out there and try. The fact that you are brave enough to even try to compete is proof that martial arts is not just changing you physically, but mentally as well.

Many of us signed up for Tae Kwon Do because we wanted more confidence in one way or another. When I see a student sign up to compete, that means more to me than any trophy that he or she could bring back to the Do Jang, because I know that I am doing my job right. I have helped him or her achieve self-confidence.

How Good Are You Anyway?

What's nice about tournaments, especially fighting, is that it lets you know where you stand skill-wise. If you can fight with someone who has close to the same amount of martial arts training that you do, and you do pretty well against him, just imagine what you could do to someone with absolutely no training at all. (Remember, of course, that street-fighting is without any rules or regulations.)

Fighting in competition is about as close as you can get to a real fight without risking bodily harm. You'll feel a little nervous and a little scared, but those are two feelings you need to know well should a real fighting situation ever arise.

Battling those Feelings

Now you know that winning and losing isn't the main objective, but there couldn't be a worse feeling for the martial artist than the one you get the evening after a tournament when you remember how badly you lost that match. As you hit the shower you can't help but ask yourself, "Why didn't I kick more? Why didn't I stay in closer?" Or, my favorite question, "Why did I just stand there and let her hit me?"

As you head out the door for your next class, you start thinking up clever answers to that one question you dread having to answer to you classmates, "How did you do?" You could say, "Well, I lost, but I had a really good time." Yeah right. Or, "I got fifth place" (since there is no *fifth place*, this one works well with non–martial artists). But the best answer really is, "I got my butt handed to me on a silver platter." Then laugh about it and forget it. There is always next time. Don't dwell on the past!

Stop making excuses and stop beating yourself over the head. It's just one tournament in a hundred that you could compete in if you wanted to, and if you do compete in a hundred tournaments, you'll eventually win something somewhere, because it's a numbers game half the time anyway.

Second-Guessing Yourself

Point fighting is a great way to see where you need to sharpen your sparring skills, but it has very little to do with the real thing. Scoring a couple of points in a two-minute period has nothing to do with what you could do to that person if he really accosted you on the street (remember, no rules on the street). So don't go off thinking that you'll be killed in a real fight just because you got beaten in the tournament. If you are halfway good at your Tae Kwon Do, you've already got the edge on the street.

> **Martial Arts Minute**
> Different parts of the country have different ways of conducting tournaments. Not only are the rules different, but in some competitions there are just three places while others have four, called first, second, and two thirds (those who lose the last two matches share that third designation while the winners fight for first and second). Some tournaments even give consolation prizes like a little medallion or a patch to everyone who enters.

It's Not Fair!

There are normally only three or four winners per division, so let's face it, that's going to exclude you or your child. If you are a parent worried about equal treatment of your child and the fairness of a tournament, then don't even put your kid in there. Everyone is simply not going to place. Most competitors are going to lose, whether it seems fair or not. Of course it is fair because everyone has a fair chance at winning, but try to explain that to a crying eight-year-old.

And although the judges try to be fair, we have to admit that sometimes it just isn't. Maybe if Tae Kwon Do had instant replay we could see if that kick really was on target, but as long as we depend on the eyes of human judges, there are going to be mistakes. As long as you and your child understand this, then hand him his little mouthpiece and send him on into battle. Otherwise, spare him the agony of waiting around for sometimes literally hours with little food or water, just to come home disappointed and empty-handed. You have to be ready and willing to put up with the possible unfairness of a tournament situation.

Making the Most of Your Day

The following are things that you can do so your day of competition is a fun and valuable experience rather than a day you'd rather forget.

➤ Don't depend on winning. The power of positive thinking is good, but remember that some things in competition are out of your control. Just because you're good enough to win doesn't mean that you will win. If you live and die by a game then its going to be tough to get through life.

➤ Congratulate the winners. Immediately after trophies have been given, go up and shake the hands of the winners. Congratulate them and share in their joy, after all, they couldn't have won without you being there. Sometimes seeing the joy in someone else's face will melt away the immediate feelings you might have of envy or of being a loser.

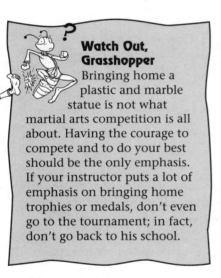

Watch Out, Grasshopper
Bringing home a plastic and marble statue is not what martial arts competition is all about. Having the courage to compete and to do your best should be the only emphasis. If your instructor puts a lot of emphasis on bringing home trophies or medals, don't even go to the tournament; in fact, don't go back to his school.

➤ Keep things in perspective. You may have heard the saying "losing hurts worst than winning feels good." When you lose, you may feel like the world is shining a huge spotlight on you, but the truth is, you're the only one putting the spotlight on yourself. Hey, nobody really cares. The spectators and even your fellow students will soon forget you lost just as you'll forgot the hundreds of other competitors who lost that day. Even the professional athletes who lose a big game realize its just that—a game!

➤ Keep your energy useful. It's the darndest thing, but when you take the time to help your junior belt classmates win, and they do win, you can't lose. They may take home the trophy, but in your heart, you have the trophy, because they couldn't have won without you. That can feel 10 times better than if you would have won the trophy yourself.

The Least You Need to Know

➤ Competitions are relatively new to the world of martial arts.

➤ Tournaments can be big or small, open to everybody or closed for just a particular school or organization.

➤ Full-contact tournaments are best left to professionals.

➤ Although winning is great, your goal should be doing your best and learning something new.

➤ Never complain that it's "not fair" if you lose. Make the most of it by congratulating the winners.

Chapter 24

Rules of the Game

In This Chapter

➤ Learning the rules of open point competitions

➤ Knowing what not to do to avoid penalties

➤ Learning the rules of Olympic competitions

➤ Learning the symbols given by the officials

➤ Learning the weight divisions of Olympic competitions

In the beginning, competition never was and still should never be the primary goal for the martial artist. We have to acknowledge, however, that for many people it is. And with Tae Kwon Do being an Olympic event, it certainly has the attraction as an international sport.

As we mentioned in the last chapter, there are several different types of tournaments where you can test your abilities against other students of the martial arts. As a result there are different sets of rules and regulations that you'll have to know and follow depending on the type of competition you find yourself in. So, here are some of the rules of the Tae Kwon Do game.

Open Competition

Just so you know, we're going to be talking about point-competitions right here, not full-contact bouts. Different federations and different parts of the country have different rules. Sometimes you can kick in the groin and sometimes you can't. Sometimes you get one point for a kick but sometimes you get two. So, as you can see right up front, we can't give you a definite set of hard and fast rules for open tournaments all across the nation.

We can give you some general rules of thumb though. A *score* is when you execute a good technique with light contact to someone's target areas. Target areas in a tournament, by the way, vary a little from the targets for self-defense that were listed back in Chapter 12, "Striking Out on Your Own." You see, it is just too easy to really hurt someone by kicking her in the knee or sticking your fingers into her eyes. For that reason, these target areas are off-limits in a tournament.

Because kicks are harder to throw than punches, some tournaments give two points for kicking techniques and just one point for hand techniques like punches, chops, and ridgehands. And since groin kicks are easier to sneak in than a good heel kick to the back of the head, some federations award more points for the more difficult kicks.

Open Competition Penalties

There is also a rule in most open competitions that states children cannot hit each other in the face or throat. In fact, you can lose a point for such contact, but there needs to be verification from a majority of judges who saw the contact. If only one judge says the punch hit the face, for example, while the other two say it was actually a point for the puncher, the result is the majority rules and it stands as a point earned rather than as a penalty point for the receiver. Adult rules are usually more lenient, with light contact to the face allowed.

A bloody nose or swollen lip usually means instant disqualification. There does not need to be a majority verification for disqualification if the kid is bleeding—it is obvious he got hit. Even adults can be disqualified for excessive contact, so be careful if you tend to be over zealous.

Black belts, by the way, can hit each other pretty hard in the face in point-competition without a warning from the judges. But even in black belt divisions, if it looks like one competitor is trying to hurt the other guy, the judges will call for a penalty point or even disqualification.

In some parts of the country, groin kicks mean loss of point, while in other states you can kick someone between the legs (both guys and girls divisions) and earn a point. Know the rules before your match starts.

Fouls and Warnings

Besides losing points for hitting the other guy in a place you're not supposed to, you can give up points by ignoring warnings from the referee. Warnings are usually handed out for things like unsportsman-like conduct (name-calling and back-talking), running out of bounds on purpose (to avoid fighting), and illegal techniques (like elbows, knees, and finger spears).

Usually they give you two warnings or fouls and then deduct a point for every foul after that. That means you can easily lose a match by just running out of bounds and accidentally kicking your opponent in the lower leg. So even if the other guy never lays a glove (or boot) on you, you can go home disappointed.

Martial Arts Minute
In the beginning there was no separation of belt ranks for women in the 1960s. There just weren't enough women entering tournaments in those days to break the division up. Often you had just a handful of competitors ranging from white belts to black belts. Even today, women's categories will tend to run together when there aren't enough to make a full division.

Two Minutes Is All You've Got

Generally speaking, a tournament match lasts just two running minutes. Running minutes means they don't stop the time unless someone's mouthpiece falls out and they have to chase it across the ring or someone faints and they have to revive him.

That means everything moves really fast. Sometimes you even lose track of the score in the midst of all the excitement. Try to stay focused and concentrate on the task at hand, scoring some more points! The time-keeper yells, "time" or sometimes even throws a white towel into the ring to signify the end of regulation time.

If the score is tied at the end of regulation, the competitors go into an overtime period where the first point wins. Overtime is especially exciting and stressful, so if it comes to this, really pay attention to your opponent's attack.

The Decision-Makers

In a typical open-point competition there will be three officials, a center referee and two side judges. All the officials move around the ring with the competitors in order to see the match and call out points. Only the center ref, however, has the authority to stop the match and to award points. Of course, a majority of judges must agree on the point. For example, if one judge says you kicked the guy in the chest, but the other judge couldn't see for sure, and the last judge says you missed—then no point. But if two of the three agree, then you got the score.

In the finals of some large tournaments, there is a total of five officials with corner judges sitting in chairs at the four corners of the ring. Again, a majority, or three of the five, must agree for points to be awarded. There is also a separate time-keeper and score-keeper for each ring. These people have no vote; they are there to do just what their titles suggest.

The Ring

The open competition ring varies from 18 feet square for some junior divisions to 20 to 25 feet square for adult divisions. Sometimes it is hard to tell where the ring starts and stops since tournaments can be held in every kind of location from church basements to school gyms to YMCA aerobic rooms. The edges of the ring are, therefore, marked with colored vinyl tape.

A typical open tournament ring.

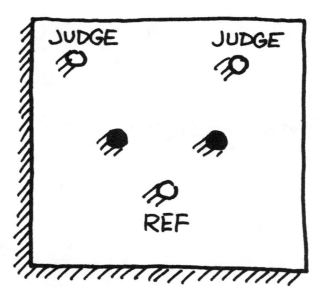

Wise Sa Bum Tells Us

Running out of the ring is one of the most disappointing ways to lose a match. Be aware of where you are at any given time during the bout. Be careful not to look straight down at the floor however, because that's a great time for the other guy to kick you.

Divisions

Kids get their own divisions, and adults are divided by gender, rank, and weight. Different tournaments have different classes for children, so we can't get too specific here, but generally speaking, your kid won't have to fight someone more than one year older or younger or one rank above or below. Because there are different belt colors in different styles, sometimes they divide it up by saying beginner, intermediate, advanced, and black belts.

Men and women are likewise divided by rank and even by weight. Usually there are two to four weight divisions depending on the size of the tournament. Remember that tournaments can have as few as a dozen competitors from your own school to over a thousand at some of the big national events. That means you might have to win just a single match for a trophy or maybe nine or 10 matches at a big tournament.

> **Know the Do**
> Open tournaments usually have *kata* competitions. Kata is the Japanese word for *form*. Typically, you can only perform the pattern for your next rank level in order to make it fair for everyone.

Olympic-Style Competition

Although not all WTF (World Tae Kwon Do Federation)-sanctioned tournaments lead to the Olympics, we are going to call the rules of this federation the *Olympic* rules. Perhaps the biggest difference in open rules and Olympic rules is the elimination of hand techniques to the head. This has been a very difficult transition for former open competitors to make as they try to fight in Olympic-style tournaments.

The WTF came up with the no-hands-to-the-head rule to make Tae Kwon Do look different than Karate to the Olympic Committee as they tried to get their brand of martial art into the big games. Karate had been trying for longer than Tae Kwon Do to make it to the Olympics, but their vast differences of styles and rules soured the committee on that art. The WTF succeeded in convincing the Olympic officials that their system was not Karate because they only kicked to the head instead of punching. Whatever you may think of this rule, it enabled Tae Kwon Do to join Judo as an Olympic event.

A point in Olympic competition is any technique delivered with a visible shock to the body of the opponent. That means you have to whack him pretty hard in the chest protector or back of the head to earn a score. Obviously, the judges are a little more lenient with kids than with adult black belts. Target areas are pretty simple, the front of the body (between the waist and the bottom of the neck) and the head. No groin, no kidney, and no spine shots allowed.

> **Know the Do**
> *Judo*, the other Olympic martial sport, means literally *gentle way*, although if you have ever seen a Judo competitor slammed to the mat, you'd smile at that description.

The Olympic Ring

Local and regional events have a ring measuring $19^1/_2$ feet square with an outside boundary marked off at 26 feet. International events have a larger ring measuring 26 feet square with an outer boundary of 39 feet.

The Olympic competition ring.

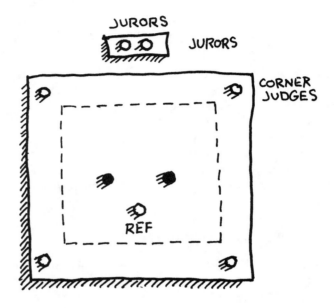

The Olympic Officials

Like in open competitions, there are a referee and side judges. All tournaments, however, have four side judges who sit in chairs at the corners of the ring. There is also a jury for every match consisting of one or two officials who decide on rules infractions and give the referee permission to award points. There is also a time-keeper and score-keeper.

Know the Do
After bowing to the jury and to each other, the fighters face each other again on hearing the command *jaw woo hyang woo*, which means *face each other*. When the ref wants the fighters to stop or break, he calls out *kalyeo*.

The referee, or center official, controls the match. He starts and stops the fighters, gives warnings for infractions and deducts points if needed. The ref also has a responsibility to stop the match, for example if one fighter is injured.

Some infractions include:

➤ Turning your back and running

➤ Stepping out of bounds

➤ Knee strike, groin attack, head punch, or verbal offense

➤ Declaring a winner

- REFEREE SIGNALS

BOW TO EACH OTHER

ROUND ONE

TIME OUT

The ref's signals: Bow to each other round one time out.

- SOME INFRACTIONS

TURNING BACK & RUNNING

STEPPING OUT OF BOUNDS

KNEE STRIKE

GROIN ATTACK

HEAD PUNCH

VERBAL OFFENSE

DECLARING
A WINNER

What to Wear to the Game

As we have said previously, the Olympic padding is a little different than the open-style protective gear. Contestants are to wear headgear, mouthpiece, chest protector, forearm and shin guards (only in white), and guys wear a cup. The standard white dobak is required, and it had better be clean and pressed. No colored trim is allowed except for black for the black belts. Sleeves can't be rolled up.

Jewelry is a bad idea and therefore isn't permitted (tell your spouse the judges made you take off your wedding ring). You can't wear glasses either, so you had better get some contact lenses or safety glasses if you can't see what the other guy is throwing your way. You are only allowed two layers of tape on your hands or feet.

Dividing Everyone Up

Kids are divided by age, rank, and weight. Adults just by rank and weight. Here are the divisions.

Men's weight classes:

>Fin under 50 kg (110 pounds)
>
>Fly under 54 kg (118.5 pounds)
>
>Bantam under 58 kg (127.6 pounds)
>
>Feather under 64 kg (140.8 pounds)
>
>Lightweight under 70 kg (154 pounds)
>
>Welter under 76 kg (167.2 pounds)
>
>Middle under 83 kg (182.6 pounds)
>
>Heavy over 83 kg

Women's weight classes:

>Fin under 43 kg (94.6 pounds)
>
>Fly under 47 kg (103.4 pounds)
>
>Bantam under 51 kg (112.2 pounds)
>
>Feather under 55 kg (121 pounds)
>
>Lightweight under 60 kg (132 pounds)
>
>Welter under 65 kg (143 pounds)
>
>Middle under 70 kg (154 pounds)
>
>Heavy over 70 kg (154 pounds)

Children's weight classes:

>**Pee Wee** (six to 12 years old)
>
>under 60 pounds
>
>under 69 pounds
>
>under 79 pounds
>
>under 89 pounds

under 99 pounds

under 109 pounds

under 119 pounds

over 119 pounds

Junior (13 to 17 years old)

under 80 pounds

under 89 pounds

under 99 pounds

under 109 pounds

under 119 pounds

under 129 pounds

under 139 pounds

under 149 pounds

under 159 pounds

over 159 pounds

Americans versus Orientals

Some of the most recognizable stars of open "Karate" tournaments have been Korean stylists. Chuck Norris, Allen Steen, Skipper Muline, and Pat Burleson were all world champions in the 1960s. Jeff Smith and Roy Kurbah were international stars in the 1970s and were Tae Kwon Do practitioners. Linda Denley and George Chung won their world titles in the '80s. Of course the Olympics have also had their share of stars.

Although the Koreans have naturally dominated the Olympic Tae Kwon Do competitions, there have been a number of Americans who have done very well. Arlene Limas, Dana Hee, Lynette Love, and Jimmy Kim all won gold medals at the 1988 Olympics. Herb Perez won his gold medal in 1992.

The Least You Need to Know

➤ In open competitions you'll usually get two points for kicks and one point for a hand technique.

➤ In Olympic-style competitions they don't allow punches to the head or face.

➤ Most tournaments have a rule that children cannot hit to the face.

➤ You can actually lose points by committing infractions.

➤ Kids are divided by age, rank, and weight. Adults just by rank and weight.

Chapter 25

T-Day: The Day of the Tournament

In case you haven't realized by now, the average Tae Kwon Do student is not going to end up on the platform at the Olympics. But you can achieve some of those same feelings of glory, if not for your country, at least for your local Do Jang and for yourself.

However, hanging that medal around your neck or putting that trophy on the mantle seems a long way away when you first walk into that gymnasium or convention center or hotel ballroom where your first tournament is being held. Let's talk about some of the things you'll face and some things you won't at a typical martial arts tournament.

Please note here that we're basically talking about the local Karate tournaments down the road that are in good standing with your own organization, and to which you've been given permission to attend.

Sleepless in Your Bed

Let's go back to the night before. Every athlete needs a good eight hours of sleep, especially when he or she will be competing pretty much all day long. Right? Don't count on it. Your body will be willing, but your mind just won't let you. Did I practice my form enough times in class? Should I change my sparring moves? These are just a few of the questions that will be dancing in your head all night long. Try to get a good night's rest, though, because falling asleep just before they call your name can be a bummer. In spite of your lack of sleep, your body will usually pull through for you when it's time to compete.

Wise Sa Bum Tells Us

Whatever film you may have seen with a tournament in it, forget it. Tournaments are seldom as glamorous as they seem when Jean Claude or Chuck is out there doing back kicks to the villain. But if they aren't as exciting with a huge cheering crowd and heart-pounding soundtrack in the background, neither are they as bloody and brutal. Your few minutes in the ring will be exciting all right, but it might take four hours of sitting on your butt till you get in there.

Snap, Crackle, Pop

Trying to eat when you know you have to fight will be a challenge in itself. A good idea is to bring something with you to snack on. Another good idea is to bring sports drinks. They're loaded with potassium and other nutrients that can sub for a meal if necessary. Power bars and fruit will also do the trick. If you have a nervous stomach, stay away from dairy products or basically stay away from the whole concept of breakfast. Believe me, you'll pay for it later, and it seems there's never any toilet paper at these events!

Watch Out, Grasshopper

They will have concession stands at tournaments but make sure your stomach can handle hot dogs and potato chips before a competition.

Early to Rise

They're usually lying when they say, "starts at nine o'clock." On the other hand as soon as you take your time and wander in at 10, they may have already finished your division. So just set your alarm (remember you probably won't be sleeping anyway), and get up, get ready, and get down there on time.

Eliminations are normally 10 or 11 A.M., but if you haven't pre-registered, you'll have to get there early to register too.

A word of warning about driving: Once you locate the facility, nine times out of 10 it's "good luck finding a place to park." Finally, you see the line winding down the next block for registration, you'll know why we said "get there early."

Where Are the Facilities?

So you've finally paid your entry fee and it's off to the locker room to get changed. All the while you're looking around to see those on the floor with the same colored belt as yours. As you get dressed, you sort of mumble a half-hearted "Hi" to the others, wondering if it's someone you'll be meeting later in the ring.

Finding a place to put on your uniform can also be a problem. It depends on where the event is being held, but imagine a hundred women trying to change into their dobaks in a three-stall hotel bathroom. Many people just wear their uniform pants and a T-shirt, so changing won't be a problem. (Of course guys then have to put their cups on and wear them for 14 hours straight as well.)

Wise Sa Bum Tells Us

By the way, though you'll be competing in your bare feet, you may want to wear your shoes around until that time since the floor may not be as clean as what you're used to in your own Do Jang.

Since you won't know what kind of flooring the competition area will have (sometimes it's carpet but other times it may be tile flooring—slippery tile flooring), be prepared. (The possibility of slipping and falling is one reason why tournament promoters require foam helmets for all competitors.) Ladies, forget about softening your feet up with lotion in the morning. This can greatly change the patterns of your form when you start sliding all over the ring.

Relax and Wait

Okay, you're changed and ready to go. Now what do you do? Start heading out to the floor for stretching and warm-ups. It's absolutely fascinating to see the others warming up, especially at an open tournament. All the different uniforms and weapons...I've had several students drop out of competition right at this point!

Believe me, they're just as scared as you are. Nobody knows what to expect from you, just as you don't know what to expect from them. Keep cool. And don't overdue the practice thing. Just stretch, maybe go over a couple of moves in your form. Don't give away any of your *secret weapons* because if you don't know your stuff by now, you won't know it any better in the next couple of hours.

269

Line Up, Finally!

Finally the tournament director will call the event to order (if it was scheduled for 11 A.M., it's probably now 12:30). At least you think that's what he said. Between the broken English and the misuse of the microphone, listening for audio cues can really get challenging. Keep in mind that you'll have to line up according to rank just like in class for the opening ceremonies. Some of those uniforms are creative; you may have to ask what someone's rank is just to find out where you need to go. If they say something like "I'm at the checkered rank of the third dragon," restate the question, this time asking how many years he or she has been training.

Once in line, get ready for the worst rendition of the national anthem you've ever heard in your life. It's usually sung by a lower-ranked student who felt threatened, or a student who is being punished for bad behavior. If they play it off a cassette you're in luck. Normally the anthem of the country where the sponsoring school is from is played as well.

Now comes all the bowing and welcomes. Many times this part of the tournament is held off until somewhere in the middle of the competition. (I can recall times where I had to stand at attention in excess of an hour for this kind of event.) Finally, a few rules are explained and the ring assignments are given (hopefully by someone fluent in English).

Forms Competition

Watch Out, Grasshopper
Don't go in expecting to win, regardless of how much you've practiced. Basically you can't base your winning on the opinion of a judge who may not even understand the moves behind your style. Still, most judges are qualified black belts, and black belts can recognize good martial arts when they see it. The winners, no matter what art they do, will have a certain snap and crispness to their performance that the others seem to lack.

Usually forms competition is first. The judges assigned to your ring could be anything from a black belt who came up with his own art form in his basement, to a former champion forms competitor himself.

Here are some tips to keep in mind when you are doing forms competition:

➤ Always show respect to the judges, even if they don't reciprocate the respect.

➤ Answer loudly to your name, and yell loudly on the moves that require a yell in your form. If nothing else, you may rack up a few points for spirit.

➤ Move quickly when your name is called. A slothful student is taken as disrespectful in many art forms.

➤ If you mess up, keep going! In an open tournament, nine times out of 10, the judges aren't going to know what the heck you're doing anyway.

➤ Always bow. When in doubt, bow anyway.

So you didn't win? Well hopefully you weren't expecting to win anyway. Go up and congratulate the winners, then forget it. It's no big deal. Now start concentrating on fighting.

Are You Ready to Rumble?

Remember that tournaments vary greatly in size and intensity. Some are just between the students in your school or maybe one or two others. Other tournaments are regional affairs with several hundred competitors or even the big national and international events with thousands of people coming to compete over two days.

> **Watch Out, Grasshopper**
> Don't let someone else psych you out. Often a competitor will go around stretching and snorting just to intimidate the other entrants. Usually it's just a show. The only thing that counts is what he shows in the ring.

Separating the Men from the Boys (and Girls Too)

We've already covered some of the divisional breakdowns. Rest assured, ladies, you won't have to face a man. Children won't fight adults, but some children's divisions do allow boys and girls in the same group, since their bodies are pretty much "even-steven."

Children usually compete first in everything and are then sent home. Depending on how many competitors there are, and how long the opening ceremony drags on, sometimes you're in luck if you get around to fighting by eveningfall.

Call to Action

They have finally gotten ready to start your division. If you're going to *recarb*, now's the time to do it. You have all your fighting plans ready to go…all the little tricks you've been practicing in class. You get in the ring…and you don't do any of it! It's always this way. When you're threatened, fighting becomes an instinctive thing. Whether you win or lose, half the time, you're not going to even remember what you did. I've had judges come up to me afterward and say things like "That was a great axe kick you did." And I'll reply "Did I do that?"

Are you scared when you get in there? Yes, but only initially. Once you start fighting, the fear is replaced by hope. Hope that the whole thing will be over soon.

Just for Women

Women are lucky to even get divisional breakdowns because fewer women compete. Men, as we have already said, have belt divisions, broken down into age and weight divisions. For us ladies, what you see is what you get. I've fought everything from a woman old enough to be my grandmother to someone twice my size (a former *American Gladiator* champion).

Know the Do
What if you're worried about getting hurt? I'd be lying if I guarantee you won't. But chances are, you won't go home with anything more than a couple of bruises, and you won't even notice those until the next morning.

There were times I was paired up with sweet-looking girls who would prance when they walk but knock the be-jeebers out of you when they hit. And other times I would get paired up to someone who looked like "Mean Joe Green" in a Karate uniform only to discover that she was usually out of breath before the two minutes was up. You never can judge a book by its cover when it comes to a martial arts competition.

What Will You Take Home?

Let's say you placed in one of your divisions. What will you be bringing home after this day-long torture session? Anything from a broken nose to a six-foot trophy. But much more internally. As we said earlier, in spite of all of the anxiety and frustration you should try and compete at least once in your martial arts career.

I've come home from tournaments with so much plastic and marble in my possession at times that I had to have some of it sent to my house. Then there were times that I truly lost—I mean I tried so hard and just couldn't pull anything off. Both situations have been rewarding to me in different ways.

The time I lost my grand-championship fight to the girl who once beat out the American Gladiators I actually felt proud. Not that I lost a close match, but because I had the courage to even get in the ring with someone twice my size with such tremendous ability. Today, when I find myself having to go through a really challenging time, I always say, "If I can fight an American Gladiator, then I can do anything."

The Least You Need to Know

➤ Try to get a good night's sleep the night before and arrive on time to the tournament.

➤ Forms competition is first. Just get out there and do your best with plenty of loud yells.

➤ Your chances of getting hurt are tiny, but your chances of learning some valuable lessons are great.

➤ You may have to wait several hours before your division is called up. Use the time to observe and learn from the other competitors.

Associations and Federations

There are literally hundreds of different associations, and we're just talking about Tae Kwon Do! We spent quite a bit of time researching, but if we left somebody out, believe me, we didn't do it on purpose.

We also want to remind you that the lack of organizational sanction doesn't mean your school is not legit. That said, however, first- or second- or third-degree black belts who are on their own without any higher master or organizational support should be checked out pretty thoroughly.

Finally, we cannot guarantee that even the groups we have listed here are above reproach. Remember, just about anyone can buy a black belt from a catalog, therefore, we encourage you to check out any organization before you get involved.

Action International Martial Arts Association
11755 Wilshire Blvd. Suite 40
Los Angeles, CA 90025

American Independent Tae Kwon Do Federation
Box 402
Christiansburg, VA 24068

American Karate and Tae Kwon Do Organization
1218 Cardigan St.
Garland, TX 75040

American Tae Kwon Do Association
6210 Baseline Rd.
Little Rock, AR 72209

Gospel Martial Arts Union
512 Laurel Ave., Suite 6
St. Paul, MN 55902

International Combat Hapkido Federation
6671 W. Indiantown Rd.
Jupiter, FL 33458

International Tae Kwon Do Association
Box 281
Grand Blanc, MI 48439

International Tae Kwon Do Federation
Draugasse 3, 1210 Aienna
Austria

KoreAmerican Tae Kwon Do Union
341 Broad St.
Manchester, CT 06040

Korean Martial Arts Instructor's Association
475 W. Silver Star Rd.
Ocoee, FL 34761

Martial Arts Congress for Education/World TKD Foundation
1313 Dolley Madison Blvd., Suite 104
Mc Lean, VA 22101

Unified Tae Kwon Do International
9-405 Circle Dr.
Saskatoon SK S7K-4B4,
Canada

United States National Tae Kwon Do Federation
9956 W. Grand Ave.
Franklin Park, IL 60131

United States Tae Kwon Do Association
220 E. 86th St.
New York, NY 10028

United States Tae Kwon Do Federation (affiliated with ITF)
6801 West 117th Ave.
Broomfield, CO 80020

United States Tae Kwon Do Union (affiliated with WTF)
1750 E. Bolder St., Suite 405
Colorado Springs, CO 80909

World Hwarang Do Association
8200 Firestone Blvd.
Downey, CA 90241

World Kido Association
36472 Fremont Blvd.
Fremont, CA 94536

World Kuk Sool Won Association
3347 FM 1960 West
Houston, TX 77068

World Tae Kwon Do Federation
635 Yuksamdong
Kangnamku, Seoul 135-080
South Korea

Publications and Sources

Please note the following is a list of publications that a reader of a book on Tae Kwon Do would be interested in. It's not necessarily a complete list of martial arts publications.

Publications

Black Belt Magazine (also publishes *Karate/Kung Fu Illustrated* and *MA Training*)
Box 918
Santa Clarita, CA 91380-9018
805-257-4066

Inside Karate Magazine (also publishes *Inside Kung Fu*)
4201 W. Van Owen Pl.
Burbank, CA 91505
818-845-2656

Journal of Asian Martial Arts
821 West 24th St.
Erie, PA 16502
800-455-9517

Martial Arts Professional Magazine
3950 3rd St. North
St. Petersburg, FL 33703
800-973-6734

Tae Kwon Do Times Magazine
1423 18th St.
Bettendorf, IA 52722
319-359-7202

Resources

Asian World of Martial Arts
11601 Caroline Rd.
Philadelphia, PA 19154
800-345-2962

Century Martial Arts Supply
1705 National Blvd.
Midwest City, OK 73110
800-626-2787

Double Dragon Martial Arts Supply
5654 Van Nuys Blvd.
Van Nuys, CA 91401
888-766-5656

Golden Tiger
801 S. Dupont Ave.
Ontario, CA 91761
800-331-5367

Kim Pacific Trading Co.
4141 Business Ctr.
Fremont, CA 94538
800-227-0500

Panther Video
1010 Calle Negocio
San Clemente, CA 92673
800-332-4442

Macho Products
10045 102nd Ter.
Sebastian, FL 32958
800-327-6812

Otomix
3691 Lenawee Ave.
Los Angeles, CA 90016

Pacific Rim Products
3500 Thomas Rd., Bldg G
Santa Clara, CA 95054
800-824-2433

Tae Kwon Do Enterprises
1423 18th
Bettendorf, IA 52722
800-388-5966

Glossary

The main difficulty in putting together a glossary of terms is that there is no direct translation for some words into English. Not only that, some of the sounds in the Korean language don't translate well. For example a "j" sound as in "jelly" could also be translated "chelly." And a "d" sound as in "door" could sometimes be translated "toor." It just kind of depends on who is doing the translating. So we are going to use the most common spelling for some of these Korean words. In some cases where the Japanese term is widely used, we'll even include that too.

American Karate An eclectic blend of traditional Asian forms of Karate-like arts. While such an integration of philosophies and techniques is not unique to the United States, Americans have popularized this approach during the last half of the 20th century. Korean-based stylists often use the term "American Tae Kwon Do."

Ap chagi (Korea) "Front kick."

Ap chaolligi (Korea) "Front rising kick." A stretching leg lift.

Ap sogi (Korea) "Front balance."

Bandae chirugi (Korea) "Reverse punch."

Bandae dollyo chagi (Korea) "Reverse turning kick."

Bandal son (Korea) "Arc hand" or ridgehand.

Bodhidharma The Indian monk who supposedly went to the Shaolin Monastery in China around 525 A.D. and formulated a series of exercises that evolved into temple boxing or Kung Fu.

Bokboo (Korea) The point at which your ki power is centered, also the abdominal target area.

Budo (Japan)   "Way of fighting." A generic term referring to the contemporary Japanese martial arts which have more of a psychological emphasis than the older warrior arts known as Bujutsu.

Bushido (Japan)   "Way of the warrior." The code of behavior of the Samurai, first formulated during the peaceful times of the Tokugawa shogunate (1603–1886). It placed great emphasis on duty and loyalty to the Samurai's lord.

Centering   A concept found in all martial arts referring to a calmness and balance of mental and emotional energies. If you are centered, you are relaxed, yet alert. The center of the body is a point about two inches below the navel.

Cha bapi (Korea)   "Stomp."

Cha busigi (Korea)   "Smashing kicks." A collective term for the most powerful Tae Kwon Do kicks.

Cha jirugi (Korea)   "Piercing" or "thrusting kick."

Cha rywk (Korea)   "Borrowed power." Training system of ancient warriors where it was thought you could borrow power from external sources such as training devices, practicing with natural objects (trees and rocks), and even homemade medicines.

Chagi (Korea)   "Kick."

Chang Hon (Korea)   "Blue cottage." The pen name of General Choi Hong Hi and the name used to refer to the training patterns he designed around traditional Karate forms.

Chang kwon (Korea)   "Heel of the hand."

Charyo sogi (Korea)   "Attention stance."

Chirugi (Korea)   "Punch." Also translated *jirugi*.

Chon ji (Korea)   "Heaven and earth." The first form of the Chang Hon school devised by General Choi Hong Hi and used by the International TKD Federation, among others.

Chong sim (Korea)   "Center of gravity."

Chongdan (Korea)   "Middle" or "center."

Chongul sogi (Korea)   "Walking stance."

Chukyo marki (Korea)   "Rising block."

Chunbi (Korea)   "Ready position." Also translated *joon bee*.

Chwa (Korea)   "Left direction."

Chyu taeryon (Korea)   "Free sparring."

Cireum (Korea)   Collective term for different types of wrestling.

Daeryon (Korea)   "Sparring." The Japanese term is *kumite*.

Dallyon joo (Korea)   "Forging post." Similar to the Japanese *makiwara*.

Dan (Japan/Korea)   "Step" or "degree." Term used for black belt rank holders. First-degree black belt is often called the first step to a higher level of learning.

Danjun (Korea)   Area just below navel which is the center of gravity and believed to also be center of energy. Japanese is *hara*.

Dee   *See* Ti.

Do (Japan/Korea)   "Way" or "path." Refers to a disciplined approach to the martial arts to achieve personal development.

Do Jang (Korea)   "The place of the way." The training hall or gymnasium. *Dojo* in Japanese. Chinese is *kwoon*.

Dobak (Korea)   "Uniform." Japanese name is *gi*. Also translated *tobok*.

Dollyo chagi (Korea)   "Turning kick." Also translated *tolryo chagi*.

Dorra (Korea)   "About face."

Dwi chagi (Korea)   "Backward kick."

Dwit bal sogi (Korea)   "Rear foot stance." Cat stance. Also translated *twitpal sogi*.

Eotgeoreo marki (Korea)   "X fist block."

Form   Series of prearranged motions used in training. Most "open" martial arts tournaments have *kata* divisions, which is the Japanese term for form. Olympic-style TKD tournaments have *poomse* divisions. Other Korean terms you might hear are *hyung* and *tul*.

Fugul sogi (Korea)   "Back stance."

Goman (Korea)   "End/stop." Japanese is *ma te*. Also translated *gu mahn*.

Gong gyuk gi (Korea)   "Attacking techniques."

Gup (Korea)   "Grade." Term for ranks below black belt. Japanese term is *kyu*.

Han bal sogi (Korea)   "One-legged stance." Crane stance.

Hanguk (Korea)   Literally "Korea." The long official term is "Tae Han Min Guk."

Hangul (Korea)   The Korean alphabet, which was introduced in 1446. The low literacy rate of the country (due in part to the previously used and very difficult Chinese characters) rose over the centuries until today Korea has one of the highest literacy rates in the world.

Hard styles   These approaches rely primarily on force-against-force rather than the yielding movements of soft styles. Hard martial arts (which often contain soft elements as well) are typified by Karate and Tae Kwon Do. Sometimes referred to as "external" styles.

Hardan (Korea) "Low level."

Himm (Korea) "Force." Also power.

Hosin Sul (Korea) "Self-defense techniques."

Hwa Rang-Do (Korea) "Way of the flower of manhood." Code of behavior of the ancient Hwarang warriors of Korea. Similar to the Japanese Bushido, code of the Samurai. Also a modern Korean martial art style.

Hyung (Korea) *See* Form.

Ilbo taeryon (Korea) "One-step sparring." A method of training in which your partner attacks with a single step, allowing you to practice your block and counterattack. Used in most martial systems. Japanese is *ippon kumite*.

Jang kwan nim (Korea) "Honored headmaster." Refers to the founder or headmaster of a kwan (school).

Jeja (Korea) "Student."

Jeum (Korea) "Point." As in a competition score.

Jip joong (Korea) "Concentration."

Joo sim (Korea) "Referee."

Judo (Japan) Usually translated "gentle way." Founded in 1882 by Jigoro Kano, a Jujutsu master. Based on overcoming an opponent's attack by using his strength against him by twisting and turning your body. Utilizes many sweeps and throws. The atemi-waza (striking techniques) are used only for self-defense and not in competition. Judo was the first martial art to be recognized as an Olympic sport in 1960.

Jujutsu (Japan) "Art of flexibility," "art of suppleness," or "art of gentleness." Unlike its softer offspring Judo, Jujutsu utilizes a lot of striking and blocking in its arsenal of throws, chokes, and joint-locks.

Kagup (Korea) "Rank."

Kalyeo (Korea) "Break." As in "stop fighting" during a competition.

Kara "Empty" or "China." Japanese pronunciation of either of two ideograms pared with "te" to create Karate. Originally "kara" (China hand) was used, but Gichin Funakoshi reportedly changed the word to "empty hand."

Karate (Japan) "Empty hand."

Keeoh dah (Korea) "Change sides."

Ki (Korea/Japan) "Spirit," "breath," or "vital energy." Energy created from a combination of proper breathing, mental concentration, and physical technique. Known as *chi* in Chinese martial arts.

Kiap (Korea)   "Spirit meeting." The yell of the martial artist which is said to concentrate the physical, mental, and spiritual energies all together. *Kia* in Japanese.

Kima sogi (Korea)   "Riding stance."

Kimchi (Korea)   A picked vegetable that is a staple of the Korean diet. Usually a strong-smelling cabbage or cucumber. You may be invited to eat it at a Korean celebration.

Kukkiwon (Korea)   The headquarters of South Korean–style TKD located in Seoul, South Korea.

Kung Fu (Chinese)   "Skill," "strength," or "task." Literally means a strength or skill to do a certain task. Has come to be a generic term to designate the Chinese martial arts.

Kupso (Korea)   "Vital points."

Kyokpa (Korea)   "Breaking."

Kyungye (Korea)   "Bow." Also translated *kyong ye*.

Ma sogi (Korea)   "Closed stance."

Marki (Korea)   "Block." Also translated as *makgi*.

Mudo Do Jang (Korea)   "Military" training hall. You know Do Jang means training hall; the prefix mudo is "military."

Myung chi (Korea)   "Solar plexus."

Ninja (Japan)   "Stealer in" or "spy." Hired assassins, terrorists, and spies in feudal Japan. Unlike the Samurai, they had no allegiance to anyone. They became legends in the 13th to 17th centuries in Japan because of their reputed skills of stealth.

Orun (Korea)   "Right direction."

Palmok (Korea)   "Forearm" or "wrist area."

Parro (Korea)   "Return." Often used in Korean martial arts classes as a command to resume the ready posture. Also translated *barryo*.

Poomse (Korea)   *See* Form.

Pressure points   Specific vital areas of the body which, when struck with minimal force, create maximum pain. The art and science of pressure points can be used for health (acupressure and acupuncture) or to cause death.

Pyugi (Korea)   "Stretching."

Pyung dan (Korea)   "Peaceful." Name for one of the early set of training patterns.

Sa Bum (Korea)   "Instructor." Korean equivalent to Japanese *Sensei*. Sometimes the suffix "nim" is added as in "Sa Bum-nim" to indicate added respect.

Samurai (Japan)   "Warrior" or "one who serves." Feudal Japanese warriors who served their lords. Codes of conduct were established for both lords and their samurai after 1600 during the Tokugawa shogunate era.

Sangdan (Korea)   "Upper level." Japan is *jodan*.

Sensei (Japan)   "Teacher" or, more literally "old one." Has come to refer to an instructor in Japanese and Okinawan martial arts. Korean equivalent is "Sa Bum." Chinese is *sifu*.

Shaolin   The Chinese temple where Bodhidharma taught his 18 exercises to the monks. Actually, there is more than one Shaolin Temple. Today there are several styles of Shaolin Kung Fu, each claiming a direct link to Bodhidharma. Shaolin styles tend to be among the "harder" styles of Kung Fu.

She gan (Korea)   "Time." As in "time out" during competition.

Shejak (Korea)   "Begin." Japanese is *hajime*.

Shio (Korea)   "At ease." Sometimes translated *shuot*.

Simsa (Korea)   "Rank testing."

Soft styles   These approaches to the martial arts tend to feature yielding and "blending" movements rather than the forceful blocks and strikes of the hard styles. Sometimes also called "internal styles" because of their emphasis on "inner power." Examples would be Japanese Aikido and Chinese Tai Chi.

Sogi (Korea)   "Stance."

Sokdo (Korea)   "Speed."

Song su marki (Korea)   "Twin-handed block."

Soodo (Korea)   "Knife hand."

Tae Kwon Do (Korea)   "Way of kicking and punching."

Tae Kyon (Korea)   An ancient Korean fighting art.

Tai Chi Chuan (China)   One of the major internal styles of Kung Fu. Its slow, natural movements have made it a popular method of physical fitness in China.

Tang Soo Do (Korea)   "China hand way." Korean translation of "Karate" and one of the original martial arts brought to America in the 1950s.

Ti (Korea)   "Belt." Japanese is *obi*. Also translated *dee*.

Tul (Korea)   *See* Form.

Wu shu (China)   "National sport." The official mainland name for Chinese boxing. There are two main divisions: hard styles (Shaolin) and soft styles (Tai-Chi, Pa-Kua, or Hsing-i).

Yang (yang) (Chinese)   "Active/positive." One side of the concept of equal opposites.

Yin (yin) (Chinese)   "Passive/negative." One side of the concept of equal opposites.

Yop chagi (Korea)   "Side kick."

Yop chaolligi (Korea)   "Side rising kick." A stretching leg lift.

Yudo   Korean term for Judo.

Counting in Korean

One	Hana	**Thirty**	Sorum
Two	Dul	**Thirty-one**	Sorum hana
Three	Set	**First**	Il, Cho
Four	Net	**Second**	Yi
Five	Ta sot	**Third**	Sam
Six	Ya sot	**Fourth**	Sah
Seven	Ilgup	**Fifth**	Oh
Eight	Yudol	**Sixth**	Yuk
Nine	Ahope	**Seventh**	Chil
Ten	Yul	**Eight**	Pal
Eleven	Yul hana	**Ninth**	Koo
Twenty	Sumul	**Tenth**	Sip
Twenty-one	Sumul hana		

Index

D

N-O

P

Q-R